THE SENSES

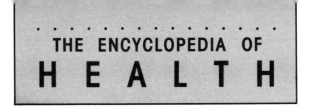

THE ENCYCLOPEDIA OF
H E A L T H

THE HEALTHY BODY

Dale C. Garell, M.D. · General Editor

THE SENSES

Mary Kittredge

Introduction by C. Everett Koop, M.D., Sc.D.
former Surgeon General, U.S. Public Health Service

CHELSEA HOUSE PUBLISHERS
New York · Philadelphia

ON THE COVER *My Sweet Rose* by John William Waterhouse
Chelsea House Publishers
EDITOR-IN-CHIEF Remmel Nunn
MANAGING EDITOR Karyn Gullen Browne
COPY CHIEF Juliann Barbato
PICTURE EDITOR Adrian G. Allen
ART DIRECTOR Maria Epes
DEPUTY COPY CHIEF Mark Rifkin
ASSISTANT ART DIRECTOR Loraine Machlin
MANUFACTURING MANAGER Gerald Levine
SYSTEMS MANAGER Rachel Vigier
PRODUCTION MANAGER   Joseph Romano
PRODUCTION COORDINATOR Marie Claire Cebrián

The Encyclopedia of Health
SENIOR EDITOR Paula Edelson

Staff for THE SENSES
ASSOCIATE EDITOR Kate Barrett
EDITORIAL ASSISTANT Leigh Hope Wood
PICTURE RESEARCHER Vicky Haluska
SENIOR DESIGNER Marjorie Zaum
DESIGN ASSISTANT Debora Smith

Library of Congress Cataloging-in-Publication Data

Kittredge, Mary
    The senses/Mary Kittredge.
      p. cm.—(The Encyclopedia of health. Healthy body)
    Includes bibliographical references.
    Summary: Discusses the five senses, the structure and function of the sensory
organs, their interrelationship with the brain and nervous system, and dysfunctions
and problems of the senses.
    ISBN 0-7910-0027-3
          0-7910-0468-6 (pbk.)
    1. Senses and sensation—Juvenile literature. [1. Senses and sensation.] I.
Title. II. Series.   89-13996
QP434.K57 1990   CIP
612.8—dc20   AC

CONTENTS

The goal of the ENCYCLOPEDIA OF HEALTH *is to provide general information in the ever-changing areas of physiology, psychology, and related medical issues. The titles in this series are not intended to take the place of the professional advice of a physician or other health care professional.*

THE ENCYCLOPEDIA OF
HEALTH

PREVENTION AND EDUCATION: THE KEYS TO GOOD HEALTH

C. Everett Koop, M.D., Sc.D.
former Surgeon General,
U.S. Public Health Service

The issue of health education has received particular attention in recent years because of the presence of AIDS in the news. But our response to this particular tragedy points up a number of broader issues that doctors, public health officials, educators, and the public face. In particular, it points up the necessity for sound health education for citizens of all ages.

Over the past 25 years this country has been able to bring about dramatic declines in the death rates for heart disease, stroke, accidents, and, for people under the age of 45, cancer. Today, Americans generally eat better and take better care of themselves than ever before. Thus, with the help of modern science and technology, they have a better chance of surviving serious—even catastrophic—illnesses. That's the good news.

But, like every phonograph record, there's a flip side, and one with special significance for young adults. According to a report issued in 1979 by Dr. Julius Richmond, my predecessor as Surgeon General, Americans aged 15 to 24 had a higher death rate in 1979 than they did 20 years earlier. The causes: violent death and injury, alcohol and drug abuse, unwanted pregnancies, and sexually transmitted diseases. Adolescents are particularly vulnerable because they are beginning to explore their own sexuality and perhaps to experiment with drugs. The need for educating young people is critical, and the price of neglect is high.

Yet even for the population as a whole, our health is still far from what it could be. Why? A 1974 Canadian government report attributed all death and disease to four broad elements: inadequacies in

7

the health care system, behavioral factors or unhealthy life-styles, environmental hazards, and human biological factors.

To be sure, there are diseases that are still beyond the control of even our advanced medical knowledge and techniques. And despite yearnings that are as old as the human race itself, there is no "fountain of youth" to ward off aging and death. Still, there is a solution to many of the problems that undermine sound health. In a word, that solution is prevention. Prevention, which includes health promotion and education, saves lives, improves the quality of life, and, in the long run, saves money.

In the United States, organized public health activities and preventive medicine have a long history. Important milestones include the improvement of sanitary procedures and the development of pasteurized milk in the late 19th century, and the introduction in the mid-20th century of effective vaccines against polio, measles, German measles, mumps, and other once-rampant diseases. Internationally, organized public health efforts began on a wide-scale basis with the International Sanitary Conference of 1851, to which 12 nations sent representatives. The World Health Organization, founded in 1948, continues these efforts under the aegis of the United Nations, with particular emphasis on combatting communicable diseases and the training of health care workers.

Despite these accomplishments, much remains to be done in the field of prevention. For too long, we have had a medical care system that is science- and technology-based, focused, essentially, on illness and mortality. It is now patently obvious that both the social and the economic costs of such a system are becoming insupportable.

Implementing prevention—and its corollaries, health education and promotion—is the job of several groups of people.

First, the medical and scientific professions need to continue basic scientific research, and here we are making considerable progress. But increased concern with prevention will also have a decided impact on how primary care doctors practice medicine. With a shift to health-based rather than morbidity-based medicine, the role of the "new physician" will include a healthy dose of patient education.

Second, practitioners of the social and behavioral sciences—psychologists, economists, city planners—along with lawyers, business leaders, and government officials—must solve the practical and ethical dilemmas confronting us: poverty, crime, civil rights, literacy, education, employment, housing, sanitation, environmental protection, health care delivery systems, and so forth. All of these issues affect public health.

Third is the public at large. We'll consider that very important group in a moment.

Fourth, and the linchpin in this effort, is the public health profession—doctors, epidemiologists, teachers—who must harness the professional expertise of the first two groups and the common sense and cooperation of the third, the public. They must define the problems statistically and qualitatively and then help us set priorities for finding the solutions.

To a very large extent, improving those statistics is the responsibility of every individual. So let's consider more specifically what the role of the individual should be and why health education is so important to that role. First, and most obviously, individuals can protect themselves from illness and injury and thus minimize their need for professional medical care. They can eat nutritious food, get adequate exercise, avoid tobacco, alcohol, and drugs, and take prudent steps to avoid accidents. The proverbial "apple a day keeps the doctor away" is not so far from the truth, after all.

Second, individuals should actively participate in their own medical care. They should schedule regular medical and dental checkups. Should they develop an illness or injury, they should know when to treat themselves and when to seek professional help. To gain the maximum benefit from any medical treatment that they do require, individuals must become partners in that treatment. For instance, they should understand the effects and side effects of medications. I counsel young physicians that there is no such thing as too much information when talking with patients. But the corollary is the patient must know enough about the nuts and bolts of the healing process to understand what the doctor is telling him. That is at least partially the patient's responsibility.

Education is equally necessary for us to understand the ethical and public policy issues in health care today. Sometimes individuals will encounter these issues in making decisions about their own treatment or that of family members. Other citizens may encounter them as jurors in medical malpractice cases. But we all become involved, indirectly, when we elect our public officials, from school board members to the president. Should surrogate parenting be legal? To what extent is drug testing desirable, legal, or necessary? Should there be public funding for family planning, hospitals, various types of medical research, and medical care for the indigent? How should we allocate scant technological resources, such as kidney dialysis and organ transplants? What is the proper role of government in protecting the rights of patients?

What are the broad goals of public health in the United States today? In 1980, the Public Health Service issued a report aptly entitled *Promoting Health—Preventing Disease: Objectives for the Nation.* This report expressed its goals in terms of mortality and in terms of intermediate goals in education and health improvement. It identified 15 major concerns: controlling high blood pressure; improving family planning; improving pregnancy care and infant health; increasing the rate of immunization; controlling sexually transmitted diseases; controlling the presence of toxic agents and radiation in the environment; improving occupational safety and health; preventing accidents; promoting water fluoridation and dental health; controlling infectious diseases; decreasing smoking; decreasing alcohol and drug abuse; improving nutrition; promoting physical fitness and exercise; and controlling stress and violent behavior.

For healthy adolescents and young adults (ages 15 to 24), the specific goal was a 20% reduction in deaths, with a special focus on motor vehicle injuries and alcohol and drug abuse. For adults (ages 25 to 64), the aim was 25% fewer deaths, with a concentration on heart attacks, strokes, and cancers.

Smoking is perhaps the best example of how individual behavior can have a direct impact on health. Today cigarette smoking is recognized as the most important single preventable cause of death in our society. It is responsible for more cancers and more cancer deaths than any other known agent; is a prime risk factor for heart and blood vessel disease, chronic bronchitis, and emphysema; and is a frequent cause of complications in pregnancies and of babies born prematurely, underweight, or with potentially fatal respiratory and cardiovascular problems.

Since the release of the Surgeon General's first report on smoking in 1964, the proportion of adult smokers has declined substantially, from 43% in 1965 to 30.5% in 1985. Since 1965, 37 million people have quit smoking. Although there is still much work to be done if we are to become a "smoke-free society," it is heartening to note that public health and public education efforts—such as warnings on cigarette packages and bans on broadcast advertising—have already had significant effects.

In 1835, Alexis de Tocqueville, a French visitor to America, wrote, "In America the passion for physical well-being is general." Today, as then, health and fitness are front-page items. But with the greater scientific and technological resources now available to us, we are in a far stronger position to make good health care available to everyone. And with the greater technological threats to us as we approach the 21st century, the need to do so is more urgent than ever before. Comprehensive information about basic biology, preventive medicine, medical and surgical treatments, and related ethical and public policy issues can help you arm yourself with the knowledge you need to be healthy throughout your life.

FOREWORD

Dale C. Garell, M.D.

Advances in our understanding of health and disease during the 20th century have been truly remarkable. Indeed, it could be argued that modern health care is one of the greatest accomplishments in all of human history. In the early 1900s, improvements in sanitation, water treatment, and sewage disposal reduced death rates and increased longevity. Previously untreatable illnesses can now be managed with antibiotics, immunizations, and modern surgical techniques. Discoveries in the fields of immunology, genetic diagnosis, and organ transplantation are revolutionizing the prevention and treatment of disease. Modern medicine is even making inroads against cancer and heart disease, two of the leading causes of death in the United States.

Although there is much to be proud of, medicine continues to face enormous challenges. Science has vanquished diseases such as smallpox and polio, but new killers, most notably AIDS, confront us. Moreover, we now victimize ourselves with what some have called "diseases of choice," or those brought on by drug and alcohol abuse, bad eating habits, and mismanagement of the stresses and strains of contemporary life. The very technology that is doing so much to prolong life has brought with it previously unimaginable ethical dilemmas related to issues of death and dying. The rising cost of health care is a matter of central concern to us all. And violence in the form of automobile accidents, homicide, and suicide remains the major killer of young adults.

In the past, most people were content to leave health care and medical treatment in the hands of professionals. But since the 1960s, the consumer of medical care—that is, the patient—has assumed an increasingly central role in the management of his or her own health. There has also been a new emphasis placed on prevention: People are recognizing that their own actions can help prevent many of the conditions that have caused death and disease in the past. This accounts for the growing commitment to good nutrition and

11

regular exercise, for the fact that more and more people are choosing not to smoke, and for a new moderation in people's drinking habits.

People want to know more about themselves and their own health. They are curious about their body: its anatomy, physiology, and biochemistry. They want to keep up with rapidly evolving medical technologies and procedures. They are willing to educate themselves about common disorders and diseases so that they can be full partners in their own health care.

The ENCYCLOPEDIA OF HEALTH is designed to provide the basic knowledge that readers will need if they are to take significant responsibility for their own health. It is also meant to serve as a frame of reference for further study and exploration. The ENCYCLOPEDIA is divided into five subsections: The Healthy Body; the Life Cycle; Medical Disorders & Their Treatment; Psychological Disorders & Their Treatment; and Medical Issues. For each topic covered by the ENCYCLOPEDIA, we present the essential facts about the relevant biology; the symptoms, diagnosis, and treatment of common diseases and disorders; and ways in which you can prevent or reduce the severity of health problems when that is possible. The ENCYCLOPEDIA also projects what may lie ahead in the way of future treatment or prevention strategies.

The broad range of topics and issues covered in the ENCYCLOPEDIA reflects the fact that human health encompasses physical, psychological, social, environmental, and spiritual well-being. Just as the mind and the body are inextricably linked, so, too, is the individual an integral part of the wider world that comprises his or her family, society, and environment. To discuss health in its broadest aspect it is necessary to explore the many ways in which it is connected to such fields as law, social science, public policy, economics, and even religion. And so, the ENCYCLOPEDIA is meant to be a bridge between science, medical technology, the world at large, and you. I hope that it will inspire you to pursue in greater depth particular areas of interest and that you will take advantage of the suggestions for further reading and the lists of resources and organizations that can provide additional information.

AUTHOR'S PREFACE

Still Life with Plate of Food *by Giuseppe Recco*

The five senses—sight, hearing, touch, taste, and smell—are the communication systems through which human beings learn about the world around them. Through them people can appreciate the colors of a sunset, the rhythms and harmonies of music, the softness of silk, the sweetness of ice cream, and the perfume of a rose. It is easy to take the functioning of the senses for granted because when they are healthy, their transfer of information from the physical world is so smooth that it seems automatic.

But imagine for a moment what life would be like without them: no sight, only darkness; no sound, only silence; no sense of touch or balance, no difference among sitting, standing, or lying down; no smells; no tastes, just—nothing. Without the five senses, not only would the outside world disappear, but even more frightening, human beings would not even know they were alive.

The senses are not only essential information and awareness systems, they are also basic tools for survival. With their help humans find food and water; without them people would quickly starve or die of thirst. Even if food and water were placed in their mouth, people would not recognize them without taste or touch sensations and so would not know to swallow them.

Without the information the five senses provide, a person would never know of danger, much less be able to escape it. The smell of smoke from a fire, the blare of a car's horn, the sight of a cliff's edge, the bitter taste of poison, the sharpness of a knife— all would be meaningless. And because people would be unable to feel pain—a special kind of sensation that can be experienced through several of the senses—they would not even realize they were being harmed.

The senses of human beings are not as keen as those of some other animals. A male silkworm moth, for instance, can smell a female moth seven miles away, and some bats find food by emitting high-pitched squeaks, then listening for the tiny echoes that bounce off flying insects. But in some ways the human senses are amazingly perceptive: The skin can feel a touch as light as one-thousandth of an ounce (about a mosquito's weight); the nose can detect some chemicals in amounts smaller than a trillionth of an ounce; and many people can taste citric acid (the chemical that makes lemon juice taste sour) in concentrations as small as eight parts per million (a dilution of, for example, eight ounces of lemon juice in a million ounces of water).

Human sight possesses 70% of all the body's sense receptors and is remarkably sharp. In bright light the eye can see a wire one-hundredth of an inch thick from 100 yards away, and in darkness it can detect light in amounts as small as 1 quantum

Bats emit continuous supersonic sound waves too high for the human ear to register. Their highly sensitive nose and ears record the frequency at which these waves bounce off objects, allowing bats to "see" their surroundings with these organs.

(a quantum is the tiniest bit of light that can be measured with the most sensitive scientific instruments). Human ears, although not as keen as those of a bat, can detect sounds ranging from the faint clink of a pin drop to the roar of a jet engine and can distinguish between two different sounds even if they differ in intensity by as little as 1 decibel (the loudness of a whisper is about 20 decibels).

The eyes, ears, nose, mouth, and skin, then, are vital and sensitive information-gathering organs that allow human beings to receive sensory information. But this is only half the story. Once the sensory input reaches the senses, it must travel through the nervous system—a vast, branching network of special communications cells within the body—to the brain. This organ, the information-processing center of the body, sorts the raw sensory signals, makes sense of them, and actually "experiences" sensations. People see with their eyes, for example, but it is the brain that "knows" what they see; it is the brain that creates the picture they experience. With the other senses it is the same: The senses gather sensory information, but humans experience and understand these sensations through their brain.

HISTORICAL THEORIES

The connection between bodily sensation and the mind is extremely complex, and to this day some of its elements remain beyond scientific understanding. But throughout history mankind has speculated about the human senses, regarded them with wonder, and sometimes even endowed them with superstitious or religious powers. For example, many ancient societies believed the eyes to be not only organs of sight but organs of magic. One early record of this conception is a bas-relief of ancient Egyptian medical instruments, dating from around 100 B.C., depicting two pairs of "magic eyes." At one time doctors may have used such instruments to identify the evil spirits that Egyptians believed caused disease and tormented sick persons. Another instance of the association of magic with sight is found in the ancient Greek myth of Argus, the hundred-eyed monster who guarded the goddess queen Hera; when Argus was slain by Hermes, the queen honored her deceased guardian by adorning the tail of the peacock with his eyes.

Eyes have also been invested with evil powers. In Russia as recently as 1881, the Russian Academy of Sciences forced a starving prisoner to stare at a loaf of bread for three days. The academy scientists then analyzed the bread and reported that it contained poison not present before the experiment. Even today, in islands of the South Pacific, in countries around the Mediterranean, in Africa, and in some isolated parts of the United States, people continue to believe that a glance from the "evil eye" can bring misfortune or death.

Ancient societies associated magic or religious properties with the senses of hearing, smell, taste, and touch as well. In ancient Greek mythology, sailors who heard the song of the Sirens became entranced, dashed their ships upon rocks, and perished in the ocean. Frankincense, one of the gifts the three kings in the Bible brought to the newborn infant Jesus, was a substance from the sap of certain deciduous trees. Its smoke was thought to remove harmful vapors that caused diseases.

Modern society still attaches mystical properties to the senses. Some religions associate the sweetish smell of burning incense with purification. Members of evangelical faiths believe the touch of a faith healer's hand will cure disease. The consumption of "magical" herbs or fungi is thought to bring on religious "visions," especially among natives of some South American countries.

Such magical associations must stem from the air of mystery attributed to the senses, a result of their having been so little understood. To learn how they work, scientists have first had to discover complex facts about light, sound, chemistry, and the human body itself. Understanding how sight works, for example, has required knowledge not only of human anatomy (the structures of the body) and physiology (the functions of bodily structures) but also of optics (the study of light rays and how glass lenses affect them) and the very complex field of quantum physics (the study of radiant energy), which explores what light itself is and how it behaves.

In Greek mythology, Hera, queen of the gods, appointed the hundred-eyed Argus to watch over her. When Hermes lulled him to sleep with music and slew him, Hera turned Argus's eyes into ornaments on the tail of the peacock.

Another branch of science that has contributed to scientists' understanding of the way the senses function is the study of human perception, or how the mind turns the raw material that the nerves and sense organs deliver to it into "experienced" sensation. How, for instance, does the mind create a single picture from the double-vision signals delivered by our two eyes? When viewing an object in motion, how does one know it is the object that moves, rather than the backdrop behind it? Why does the emotion of fear increase the sensation of pain? Why does food that "looks good" also taste better? And why does good-tasting food improve the digestive functions of the intestines? The answers to these and many other fascinating questions about the senses lie not only in the sense organs but also in the brain itself, perhaps the most powerful component of the sensory system.

This volume will look back to explore what earlier people thought about the senses and will detail how modern knowledge about them has been acquired. It will describe the structure and function of the sensory organs—the eyes, ears, nose, tongue, and skin—along with the nervous system and the brain and examine how these systems together create sensory experience. It will also explain what may go wrong with the function of the senses and how malfunction may be prevented or treated. Finally, it will discuss recent advances in sensory research, which are leading to improved care of people with sensory-limiting disorders such as blindness and deafness.

The study of human perception will always invite further scientific inquiry, but no matter how much of the sensory system is understood, these windows onto the world can never be stripped of their fundamental mystery.

•   •   •   •

CHAPTER 1

AN OVERVIEW OF THE SENSORY SYSTEM

Patterns of color, light, and movement strike the eyes, but not until nerve signals race from eye to brain does one detect the impending danger of a speeding car headed in one's way. Sound waves bombard a human eardrum, but only the brain interprets the sound of the shrieking siren as a danger signal. Molecules of chemicals assault taste buds while smell receptors deep within the nose react, but only the brain cautions that the tea being sipped is hot.

The above examples illustrate a fundamental fact about the sensory system: The sense organs gather information, but they do not understand what they sense any more than a camera can understand pictures or an answering machine can understand what a person is saying. Nor can sense organs discriminate between important information—the smell of smoke, a cry of pain—and noncrucial background impressions such as the hum of an air conditioner or the pressure of clothes on the skin.

Not until signals from the sense organs reach the brain are they sorted and processed into the experience of sight, hearing, smell, taste, and touch. Scientists do not know everything about the way the brain creates experiences from raw sensory data, but in general they describe the process in the following way: Information gathered by the eyes, ears, nose, skin, and tongue travels to the brain through the nervous system, a network composed of special cells called nerve cells. The first step in the process occurs in the sense organs themselves, where the tiny nerve-cell endings of the sensory nerves are stimulated—in the eyes by light, in the ears by sound, in the nose and tongue by molecules, and in the skin by heat, cold, vibration, or pressure.

Once the skin is stimulated, nerve cells in the sense organs transmit minute electrical signals called nerve impulses along the nervous system pathways to the spinal cord, a ropelike structure within the protective covering of the backbone. The spinal cord sends the impulses up to the brain. In the sense of smell, signals from sensory-nerve endings in the nose move along nerve fibers through the roof of the nose directly to the brain. Chemicals called neurotransmitters regulate the electrical signals by causing the nerve impulses to jump the gap, called a synapse, between the end of one nerve (the axon) and the beginning of another (the dendrite).

THE CEREBRAL CORTEX

When an object is touched, touch receptors in the skin send signals that travel to the top of the spinal cord, into an inch-long structure at the base of the brain called the medulla, and from there into a slightly larger structure called the pons. This fibrous bridgelike area (*pons* means "bridge" in Latin) sends the impulses deep within the brain to a small plum-shaped organ called the thalamus, which sorts the impulses and routes them to the main

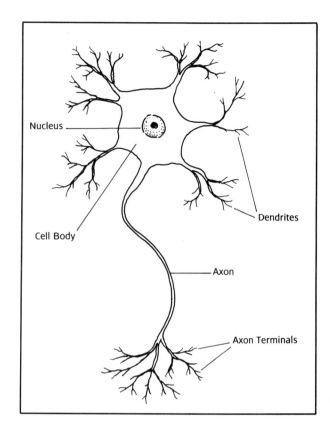

An idealized neuron. Axons and dendrites serve as essential links that allow neurons to communicate with each other. Messages are received through the dendrites and transmitted along the axon.

sensory-nerve processing area of the brain: the cerebral cortex.

The cerebral cortex is the deeply grooved outer layer of the brain. Its 8 billion nerve cells organize the nerve impulses from the senses and transform them into the sensations of sight, sound, touch, smell, and taste. The cerebral cortex, for instance, creates "pictures" from the nerve impulses that began when light waves stimulated nerve cells in the eyes.

The cerebral cortex is divided into sections. Each of these processes a specific kind of sensory information, controlling a vast number of other bodily functions. The frontal and prefrontal lobes, for instance, located behind the forehead bone, control movement and speech as well as complex thought. Just behind the frontal lobes on the left and right sides of the head are the parietal lobes; here impulses from the sense of touch are processed. Behind these, toward the rear of the skull, lie the occipital lobes, where information from the eyes is transformed into the experience of seeing. An area near the thalamus is thought to be

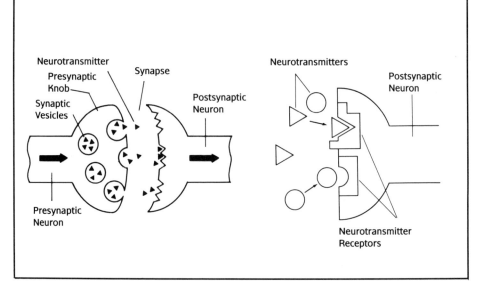

Neurotransmitter activity. The drawing on the left shows how one neuron signals another across the synapse by emitting neurotransmitters. The drawing on the right shows how each kind of neurotransmitter fits only one kind of receptor on the target neuron.

the brain's main "taste center," and toward the sides of the skull are the temporal lobes, where the centers of hearing are located.

There are two reasons why this list of "sense centers" does not even begin to suggest the tremendous complexity of what occurs in the brain when a person experiences sensations. First, people do not experience sensations one by one. Instead, they are able to see, hear, taste, smell, and touch, all at the same time. In ways that scientists are only beginning to understand, the nerve cells of the cerebral cortex communicate among themselves and with other parts of the brain to combine separate sensations into one unified experience.

A woman may simultaneously feel pressure on the soles of her feet; the movements of her arms and legs; sounds that change in rhythm, pitch, and intensity; warmth on her face; and cold sweetness on her tongue, along with many other sensations that she would not consciously note. She would never be able to decide whether or not to feel each of these sensations or to sort all these sense impressions deliberately one by one; they are simply too numerous and complex. But she does not have to: Sense organs automatically receive sensations, the nervous system transmits them, and the cerebral cortex sorts and processes them—in this instance, into the experience of walking down a sunny street while listening to a portable radio and eating an ice-cream cone.

At the same time that it sorts and processes some sense impressions, the cerebral cortex also automatically filters out a huge amount of sensory information that is neither needed nor desired. If this were not so, the amount and variety of sense input storming into the brain would be overwhelming: air movements on the skin; the millions of colors, light shades, and movements the eyes can see; the sound of traffic; even the beating of a person's own heart and the rush of air in and out of his or her lungs.

THE LIMBIC SYSTEM

Crucial to this sense-impression filtering process is a part of the brain called the limbic system, a group of structures in the parietal lobes and near the thalamus. The limbic system produces and regulates many emotions and, as noted above, is also part of the brain's "smell-processing" area. In addition, the system stimulates the cerebral cortex to notice some sensory signals with special intensity, helps to lower the intensity of other signals,

Within the brain stem, the medulla and pons sort out and direct the billions of nerve impulses traveling to and from the cerebral cortex. The cerebellum controls balance and coordination.

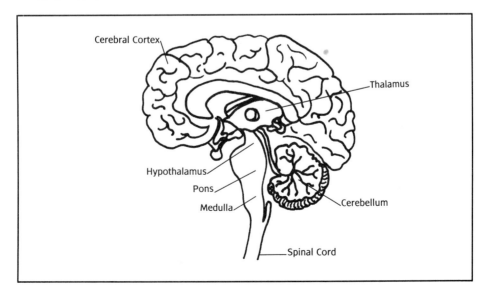

and plays a part in deciding whether signals are experienced as pleasant or unpleasant.

The limbic system has two principal ways of operating. The first way has to do with the limbic-system structure called the hippocampus. The hippocampus constantly compares incoming sensory signals to those that have passed through it earlier, the signals it has learned to "expect." (It can do so because limbic system fibers extend to many other areas of the brain and report the signals to the hippocampus.) As long as the hippocampus does not notice any new sense input, it does not stimulate the reticular formation, which is the brain area responsible for alertness. But if unusual sensory input comes in, the hippocampus signals the reticular formation, causing the cerebral cortex to pay attention to the unusual sensory signals. This, for instance, is why a person becomes instantly alert when he or she hears a strange noise. It is also why an unexpected noise sounds loud when first heard but seems to fade into the background when it is no longer considered a threat.

Right and left cerebral hemispheres. The cerebral hemispheres process sensory information, produce language, and plan movement. Here, too, originate humans' unique ability to use reason and logic.

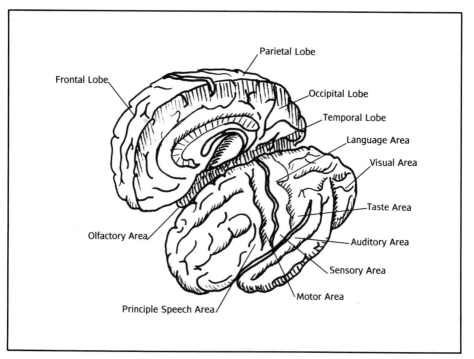

Parietal Lobe

Frontal Lobe

Occipital Lobe

Temporal Lobe

Language Area

Visual Area

Taste Area

Olfactory Area

Auditory Area

Sensory Area

Motor Area

Principle Speech Area

Other situations can also stimulate the limbic system, causing it to alert the cerebral cortex or even to change the way the cortex processes data. For instance, hunger seems to make food smell better, not because the food smell has changed, but because the limbic system's nerve fibers extend into hunger and pleasure centers in a brain structure called the hypothalamus. The hypothalamus stimulates the nerve fibers of the limbic system, and the limbic system causes the cerebral cortex to take special notice of aromas that might lead the body to food.

The second way the limbic system influences perceptions relates to the two primary functions of the system: the constant comparing of new sense information with old, through the hippocampus, and the creation and regulation of emotions, through another limbic system structure called the amygdala. The two kinds of information, emotion and sensory input, are experienced together in the same way as skin sensors may together experience heat and pressure or the tongue may sense sweet and cold at the same time. The experiences are mingled and felt together, in addition to thoughts and memories from the cerebral cortex. Thus if a person feels sad, a rainy day may look gloomy, but if he or she is happy or has pleasant memories of another rainy day, the sound of rain may be interpreted as pleasant pattering. On the other hand, the happy laughter of children may seem annoying or even provoke a fit of rage in a person who is angry because emotion generated by the limbic system affects the way the cerebral cortex perceives the sound.

SENSORY ILLUSIONS

The sense organs themselves affect sensory experience too because, like any other bodily structure, their performance is restricted to a specific range. The swiftly moving wing of a hummingbird, for instance, looks like a blur to the human eye because the eye cannot move as fast as the wing. As a result, the perception of a blur differs from what is really happening. Similarly, a very high-pitched whistle sounds like nothing at all to the human ear. The eardrum is not able to transmit extremely high-pitched sounds to nerve endings within the ear, so no information about the sound reaches the brain. Sense organs cannot gather all sensory information with perfect accuracy; they can pick up only signals that are within their range.

In the same way, the nervous system's capabilities are limited by what nerve cells are able to receive. A water molecule may land on the skin but exert too faint a pressure for the skin's nerve endings to pick it up. In such a case no nerve impulses are produced. If the nerve endings sense only a very small amount of pressure, such as that produced by a mosquito's weight, the resulting nerve impulses may be too weak for the nerves to transmit. In both cases, no nerve impulses would reach the brain, and no touch sensations would be felt, even though contact may have occurred.

Sometimes the brain organizes chaotic sense experience, or "fills in gaps," to make strange sensations fit with what it knows

The limbic system refers to the medial portion of the temporal lobe. This primitive brain structure links directly to olfaction, the processing of smell. In addition, it influences emotions, bodily responses to emotions, motivation, mood, and pain and pleasure sensations.

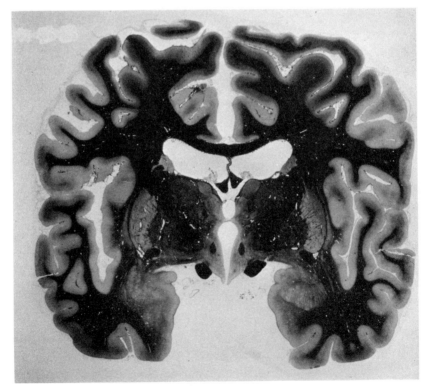

This optical illusion illustrates the brain's capacity to shift between the alternate visual patterns of two faces and a vase.

about the world. This causes sensory illusions whereby the brain's processing of the original sense information alters the sensations themselves. A simple example of a visual pattern suggesting either of two different pictures occurs in the Dutch scientist Edgar Rubin's drawing, which may be seen alternately as a vase or a pair of faces (see p. 27). An illusion from the sense of touch can be created when one person joins his or her index finger to someone else's. If the person then feels the joined fingers with the other hand, it will suddenly seem that the joined fingers no longer belong to him or her as the brain attempts to make sense of conflicting touch messages.

PERCEPTION

The process by which the human brain makes sense of "strange" sensory input continues to be a subject of debate among today's scientists. Two hypothetical descriptions of this process have gained the widest acceptance to date. According to gestalt theory, a human being's brain naturally tries to form certain basic patterns such as lines, circles, and triangles, either because these figures are "built in" to the brain somehow or because they were learned in childhood. However, another theory, called the cell theory, suggests that different cells in the brain react to different patterns of sensory input: Some brain cells are "tuned" to notice dark lines, angled lines, or slits of light, whereas others perceive changes in pitch or loudness of sound.

The question of precisely how the brain creates experience from sensation is one whose answer depends upon a great deal more research in a wide range of fields: physics (how matter and energy behave), biology (how living organisms work), psychology (how and why people think, feel, and behave the way they do), and philosophy (how ideas about the world relate to the world itself and to people's own minds), to name a few. The intricate mechanism of human perception is bound to remain a fascinating study for scientists today and for many years to come.

•　　　•　　　•　　　•

CHAPTER 2

SIGHT

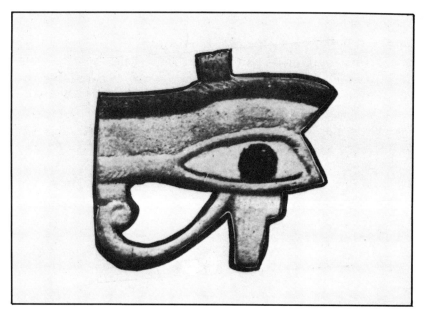

Ancient Egyptian amulet of health: the Eye of Horus

S cientists have been investigating the anatomy and physiology of the human eye for more than 2,000 years. Democritus, a Greek philosopher who lived during the 4th and 5th centuries B.C., was among the first to attempt a scientific explanation of how humans see. From his initial proposition that matter consists of atoms, he went on to surmise that objects gave off atoms that struck the eye and thereby caused it to see.

The Greek philosopher and statesman Empedocles, a near contemporary of Democritus, believed that an invisible substance radiating from the eyes caused sight. A generation later, yet another Greek philosopher, Plato, theorized that rays from the eye mingled with daylight. These rays, when combined with rays emitted by objects, caused the eye to see.

Plato's pupil Aristotle rejected the ray theory, maintaining that since such rays could not possibly reach the stars, the heavens must be seen by some other process. Instead, he suggested empty space somehow conveyed images to the eye. The Greek physician Galen, who lived during the 2nd century A.D., believed the optic nerves were channels that carried visual essences called "pneuma" from the brain; the pneuma, he said, irritated the air outside the eye. When the "excited" air touched objects, the eye saw them.

Not until about A.D. 1000 did the Arabian scientist Alhazen theorize that the eye worked like a primitive camera obscura, a device that creates a picture on a screen by allowing light to shine through a tiny hole. He correctly believed that light shone

Customers examine a spectacle maker's wares in 16th-century Frankfurt, Germany. Eyeglasses were in wide use long before scientists could explain how they worked.

through the eye's pupil, passed through a clear sheet called the lens, and produced an image on a "screen" in the eye called the retina. His was the first theory to depend not on particles emitted from the eye but on light itself.

Alhazen's accurate comparison of the eye to a camera came at about the same time as the development of eyeglasses. The English scholar Roger Bacon mentioned eyeglasses in his writings during the late 13th century, and they were in wide use by the early 14th century. Although it was soon common knowledge that glasses helped people with poor vision to see better, no one knew how or why they worked. To get a pair of glasses in that era, people simply went to the marketplace and looked through pair after pair until they found one that improved their vision.

It was not until the early 17th century that the German astronomer Johannes Kepler discovered how both the eye's lens and eyeglasses work. He realized that lenses in eyeglasses correct vision by bending light rays and that the amount the rays are bent depends on the shape and thickness of the glasses. The eye's lens itself works like a glass lens, by bending light to focus images on the retina, the eye's screen.

Eye operations had been in existence as early as the 2nd century B.C. in the Egyptian city of Alexandria. Through the centuries, the lens, the retina, the iris, and the muscles in and around the eye were discovered during operations for glaucoma (a condition of excessive pressure within the eye) and strabismus (in which one eye looks in a different direction from the other) and during enucleation (surgical removal) of an eye. But it was Kepler who first helped eye surgeons understand why their practices worked. As a result, in the 17th century the scope of knowledge of the human eye led to greater precision of surgical techniques.

The next major advance in understanding the human eye occurred when the German scientist Hermann von Helmholtz invented the ophthalmoscope in 1851, the eye-examination tool used even today. This instrument gave practical confirmation of a theory advanced by one of his contemporaries, an English scientist named Thomas Young. Young theorized that chemicals in the retina were sensitive to three colors—red, green, and violet—and that color vision depended upon these substances. This is now known as the Young-Helmholtz theory. Although this theory proved to be correct, amounts of these substances are so tiny that attempts to isolate and identify them are still being pursued by today's scientists.

In 1877 the German scientist Wilhelm Kühne made use of the ophthalmoscope to perform an intriguing experiment. After covering the eyes of a rabbit with dark cloth for 10 minutes, he withdrew the cloth and let the animal look at a barred window. Then he removed one of the rabbit's retinas, dipped it in alum (a chemical) to dry and preserve it, and examined it with an ophthalmoscope. He saw the image of the barred window at which the rabbit had been staring on the retina, as if the eye were a camera and the retina its film. Kühne already knew that the retina contained light-absorbing chemicals called rhodopsin; now he had found that light entering the eye changed the rhodopsin and that light-changed rhodopsin formed images.

By inventing the "slit lamp" microscope, the Swedish physician Allvar Gullstrand was able to see how tiny muscles, called ciliary muscles, contracted to change the shape of the eye's lens. He also observed the shape of the cornea and the way light rays are bent by the lens. In 1911, Gullstrand received the Nobel Prize in medicine for advancing scientific understanding of the relationship between light and vision in the field known as optics of the eye.

EINSTEIN AND LIGHT

By the 20th century science had amassed a great deal of information about the structure and function of the eye. However, the process of seeing involves a great deal more than the formation of chemical pictures; it was the man who revolutionized scientific understanding in the 20th century, Albert Einstein, who led scientists to understand not only the function of the eye but the mysterious nature of light itself.

In 1675, Sir Isaac Newton had claimed that light was a kind of matter made of tiny particles or "corpuscles" that shining objects such as the sun discharged. In 1690 the Dutch physicist Christiaan Huygens proposed an opposite theory: Light consisted not of solid particles but of energy "waves." In the 20th century, Einstein showed that each of these conceptions was partially true. His theory of matter and energy explained that light behaves somewhat like matter, as in the particle theory, and somewhat

Hermann von Helmholtz with the ophthalmoscope he invented in 1851. The ophthalmoscope remains an essential tool in the diagnosis of many eye disorders.

like waves, as in the energy theory, because energy and matter are different forms of the same thing, as steam and ice are different forms of water. By explaining what light was made of and how it behaved, Einstein led scientists to a clearer understanding of how light is received by the human eye. In 1921 he won the Nobel Prize in physics for his work on the theory of light.

THE ANATOMY OF THE EYE

Today, scientists know that the human eye is a globe-shaped organ made up of three layers of tissue: the tough outer coat, called the sclera (the "white" of the eye), the middle coat called the choroid, and the inner layer, the retina. A dense network of vessels between the choroid and the retina gives the eye its blood

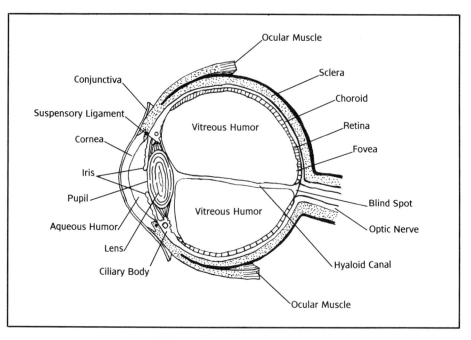

A cross section of the human eye. The proper functioning of the lens, iris, and retinal structures are essential to vision.

supply. Inside the upper eyelid, a gland called the lacrimal gland secretes lacrimal fluid, better known as tears. Six bands of muscle called the ocular muscles are attached to the eyeball, giving the eye its ability to look up, down, and around.

Inside the eye are two clear fluids: In front of the iris (the colored part of the eye) is a watery fluid called the aqueous humor, whereas the rest of the eye is almost entirely filled with the jellylike vitreous humor. The humors help the eye to hold its globe shape; without them, it would collapse inward like a deflated balloon.

The sclera, choroid, vessels, lacrimal glands, eyelids and lashes, muscles, and humors, as well as the bony eye sockets, keep the eye clean, moist, injury free, able to move, as well as in proper shape. These structures support the parts of the eye that do the actual seeing. At the front of the eye and bulging slightly outward, the sclera thins and becomes transparent to form the clear protective cornea. Light first passes through the cornea on its way into the eye.

Behind the cornea lies the aqueous humor, and behind that is the iris, a ring of colored tissue containing muscle fibers. At the center of the iris lies the pupil, the black area in the middle of the eye. The muscles of the iris control the amount of light entering the pupil. These muscles contract automatically to expose more of the pupil in dim light and relax to cover more of it in bright light. Thus, the pupil seems to enlarge in shadow and shrink in bright sunlight.

Directly behind the pupil lies a transparent round "window" of tissue called the lens, which is attached to a surrounding network of muscles called the ciliary muscle. The ciliary muscle contracts to flatten the lens or make it bulge forward so that objects come into focus on the retina.

The lens works according to the principles of optics, which describe, among other things, how light rays are affected when they pass through clear solid matter. A curved, bulging lens bends the light rays that pass through it, focusing the light reflected from nearby objects into a sharp image on the retina. A flat lens is necessary to focus light from distant objects into sharp retinal images.

The lens's ability to flatten or bulge, called accommodation, is the reason people can see both near and distant objects clearly. People who are nearsighted (for whom distant objects look blurry but near ones are clear) or farsighted (for whom distant objects look clear but near ones are blurry) have lenses that do not bulge or flatten the correct amount. They are often helped by eyeglasses or contact lenses that alter the angle at which light rays enter the eye, so light will strike the retina correctly and form a clear image there. About half the adults in the United States wear eyeglasses at least part of the time.

Once light has passed through the eye's lens, it strikes the retina, where light-sensitive cells are located. There are 2 principal types of cells: the rods (about 125 million per retina), which are responsible for black-and-white vision and vision in dim light; and the cones (about 5 million per retina), which produce color vision and detail.

The rods need only one quantum of light to see; the cones need a thousand times as much. This is why people can see only shades of gray at night; there is not enough light to trigger reactions from the cones. Located thickly at the edges of the retina and more sparsely toward the center, the rods are also responsible for peripheral vision (sight at the far right, left, top, or bottom of the "picture" our eyes see). A person can detect a moving object out of the corner of his or her eye and yet not be able to see the object precisely because the rods send only a hazy black-and-white impression and at the edges of the retina there are very few cones to fill in the color and detail.

The cones converge more thickly toward the center of the retina. They are the most tightly clustered in a spot called the macula lutea, an area of about one-tenth of an inch in diameter at the retina's center. This is why seeing straight ahead in good light produces the clearest vision and brightest colors.

Around the macula lutea are the nerve fibers that form the optic nerve. Because no cones or rods lie where the nerves pass through the retina, a "blind spot" forms through which light cannot pass. Its existence can be verified by drawing two spots on a piece of paper, the second spot about three inches from the first. When the right eye is closed and the left is focused on the right spot, the left spot will still be hazily in view. However, if one moves the paper in toward the face from an arm's length away, the left spot will seem to vanish when the paper is about 10 inches away. This will occur because light from the spot on the paper will hit the left eye's blind spot. The reason there are no "holes" in normal vision is that the brain generally "fills in the blank" of the blind spots in the left and right retinas.

THE PROCESS OF SEEING

Retinal images reach the brain through a complex chemical process. Chemicals in the retina are bound to vitamin A, a substance that is found in leafy green vegetables and liver. When isolated, the molecular structure of vitamin A forms a straight line; when it attaches to chemicals in the retina's rods (rhodopsin) and cones (opsin), it forms a curve. When light enters the eye, it breaks the bonds that hold vitamin A to the chemicals. The vitamin A then snaps back into its original straight shape, releasing in the process the energy that made it curve. Next, this energy, in the form of a tiny electrical current, travels along the rod or cone to the eye's optic nerve, stimulating it to send an impulse to the brain. The reason rods need so much less light to see than cones do is that more light is needed to break the vitamin A away from the cones' opsin than to break it away from the rods' rhodopsin.

Within the cones are three kinds of opsins; each reacts to light of different wavelengths. To understand wavelength, imagine a ray of light as a wavy line. If the line has a lot of waves close together, the distance between two waves is short; the line has a short wavelength. If the line has fewer waves farther apart, the distance between two waves is long, and the line has a long wavelength.

Natural light is a kind of energy radiated by the sun. It is part of the electromagnetic spectrum (a spectrum made up of all the kinds of energy the sun beams toward earth), and it can range from gamma rays, whose wavelength is 6 quadrillionths of an

Sensory receptor cells of the retina. Cones enable the eye to perceive color and fine detail. Rods allow vision in dim light.

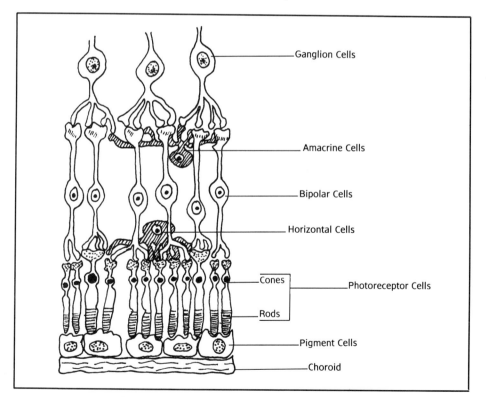

Ganglion Cells

Amacrine Cells

Bipolar Cells

Horizontal Cells

Cones

Photoreceptor Cells

Rods

Pigment Cells

Choroid

inch, to radio waves, whose wavelength may be 18 miles long. The human eye senses beams of energy with wavelengths from 400 nanometers (a nanometer is a billionth of a meter) to about 700 nanometers. These beams are what the eye experiences as light.

The mixture of light wavelengths striking the cones determines the amount of opsin involved in visual reactions. The shortest visible light rays trigger cones whose reactions the brain interprets as purple; midlength waves trigger blues and greens; long waves cause people to see reds, yellows, and oranges. When the cones work correctly, the eye can see about 7 million colors in a range from purple-black to yellow-white. When people are missing some or all of the cones' opsins, they are what is known as color blind. Some color-blind people cannot tell red from green (10% of men and 1% of women have this condition). A smaller group is unable to tell blue from yellow; and about 1 in 4,000 persons sees no colors, experiencing sight only in varying shades of gray.

Seeing movement depends in part upon the eyes' ability to move by means of contractions of the ocular muscles. There are seven kinds of eye movement. The first three are called tremor, drift, and flick; they result from the constant tension of the eye muscles on the eye. When a tiny point of light in a dark room seems to quiver, it is actually the eye that is moving. The purpose of this constant movement is to shift images around on the retina, thereby exposing fresh rods and cones and preventing fatigue.

The next two, smooth pursuit and saccadic movement, are the movements used to follow a bird in flight. Its seemingly seamless movement is really produced by a series of eye jerks as the brain estimates where the bird will be in the next instant. But the brain cannot estimate this with complete accuracy, so saccadic movement continually snaps the eye back "on target," a movement that takes only a tenth of a second.

In the sixth kind of eye movement, called vergence, the eyes turn a bit toward each other to focus together on an object, thereby preventing double vision. A person can see the effect of vergence, or the fusion of separate retinal images, by holding a pencil at arm's length and then moving it slowly toward his or her nose. When it is very near he or she will see two pencils, one with each eye, as the eye muscles can no longer bring the images together.

The viewer's ability to distinguish between near and far objects and to judge their distance is known as depth perception. The line of sight from each retina converges upon a single object, forming what is called an angle of vergence. With experience, the brain can interpret the angle of vergence, or the difference between the direction from which the image of an object reaches each retina, into a fairly accurate estimate of how far away the object is. By correlating the angle of vergence to an estimated distance, the brain adds a sense of depth and dimension to an image. Although both eyes are necessary to calculate this angle, objects viewed through one eye look similar to those seen through two because the brain is able to approximate distance through memory. But a person who has never had two eyes sees things as flat because his or her brain has no previous experience of depth perception.

The seventh eye movement, vestibulo-ocular movement, allows a person to keep an object in view even while moving his or her head or body. This ability depends upon three fluid-filled canals, called the semicircular canals, the saccules, and the utricles, buried deep within each ear. When the head moves, the fluids in these canals shift, stimulating nerves that relay information about the body's position to the brain. In response, the brain tells the eyes to move so that they remain focused on the object they are seeing.

Impulses from the retina's rods and cones travel through the optic nerves to the optic chiasma, where each nerve divides into two. Messages from the right visual fields of the left and right eyes travel to the left side of the brain, whereas left visual field messages travel to the brain's right side. Far back on both sides of the brain are the areas called the lateral geniculate nuclei, which are thought to coordinate sight messages with signals from the body's other senses. From there, the signals move to the occipital lobe at the rear of the brain.

Precisely how the brain sorts and processes visual messages into images is not known. But in general, in the occipital lobe, the striate cortex processes information about the shapes of things seen, whereas the prestriate cortex recognizes patterns.

Signals travel from there to the temporal lobe, where the brain identifies objects it has seen and helps maintain associations among sights seen now, sights seen in the past, and names of objects.

Visual signals also reach the limbic system, where visual images stimulate emotions. It is here, for instance, that the sight of impending disaster produces the emotion of fear. Sight information also travels to the cerebellum, situated below the occipital lobes, where the visual input combines with information from the body's muscles to coordinate sight and movement, as, for instance, when a ball player bats a baseball.

Much of the process of seeing depends upon physical laws, such as the way light behaves, the way chemicals respond to light, and how nerve cells transmit impulses. But the mind must also learn to see, to organize signals from the eyes into the understandable pictures humans experience. Thus, although eye

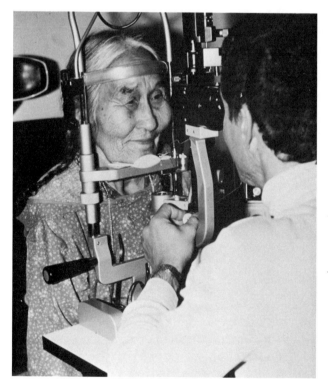

An ophthalmologist uses a portable laser to perform eye surgery on an Eskimo woman in Alaska. Its small size allows doctors to operate in remote areas where more powerful lasers are in short supply.

surgery may restore sight to a man who has been blind from birth, he may not at first see any difference between an object and its background or be able to focus on moving objects; his brain will not know how to process such information.

EYE DISEASES AND BLINDNESS

Seeing is of no use if the viewer does not know what he or she is looking at. Because the brain is the processor of all visual information, if it is injured or diseased, impaired sight may result, even when nothing is wrong with the eyes. This is the case in Kluver-Bucey syndrome. Although this condition does not affect the eyes or the nerves, it does damage the temporal lobe of the brain; because the visual signals cannot be processed completely, the sufferer is unable to recognize visual objects.

As noted above, glasses or contact lenses can improve near-sightedness (myopia) and farsightedness (hyperopia), as well as astigmatism (blurred vision due to irregularly shaped corneas). Other eye conditions include strabismus (eyes that go in different directions, resulting from weak or abnormal eye muscles) and amblyopia (one eye works less well than the other or not at all). Glasses can help these problems, as can eye exercises to improve eye-muscle strength and, in severe cases, surgery on eye muscles.

More than 15 million people in the United States have serious difficulty with their sight; more than 500,000 are blind. Four percent of all blindness results from eye injuries, which are also responsible for about 400,000 cases of permanent vision impairment each year. The most common eye injuries involve contact with pieces of loose metal. Such accidents tend to occur when metal is cut or ground at industrial jobs. The second most common cause of blindness is the careless use of contact lenses. When they are not inserted or removed properly or when they are left on the eye too long, they can wound or scar the cornea (the clear front "skin" of the eye). If improperly cleaned, they may also carry bacteria or viruses that cause scarring infections.

Luckily, corneal transplants are possible, and they succeed in restoring at least partial vision about 85% of the time. Although the source for most transplanted corneas is restricted to donors who have died within the past 24 hours, if frozen at −321 degrees

Fahrenheit, the donated cornea can be preserved for a much longer period. Cataracts, the clouding of the lens prevalent among elderly people, can also be corrected through surgery. The clouded lens is removed and replaced with an artificial one. More than 90% of these procedures are successful.

Acute glaucoma is a condition in which the drainage channels from the eye become blocked, causing fluid pressure suddenly to rise. Unless the pressure is reduced immediately—through drug therapy or surgery—it will damage the retinal cells, optic disc, and optic nerve and cause blindness. Chronic glaucoma is in many ways more dangerous than its acute form because pressure builds very gradually and so may cause damage even before recognizable symptoms appear. For this reason, doctors recommend that all people over the age of 20 be tested for glaucoma every 2 years to ensure early detection of the disease.

Cell for cell, the retina requires a larger supply of blood than any other area of the body. High blood pressure, blood clots, and other related diseases that disrupt the blood supply to the retina can cause blindness. One such condition that usually results in blindness, retinitis pigmentosa, is not well understood and at present has no cure.

But the diseases that most commonly cause blindness are age-related diabetes and macular degeneration. People with diabetes, an ailment that keeps the body from using sugar properly, often suffer severe damage to retinal blood vessels and nerves; leaking blood and damaged tissue can ruin sight permanently. In macular degeneration, the center of the retina is damaged by heat from light entering the eye; this occurs mostly in elderly persons whose eyes have been absorbing light and heat for many years. Diabetes is not currently curable, but regular doses of the hormone insulin can control it. Advanced-age macular degeneration, which affects about a third of all adults over the age of 65 to some degree, also lacks a cure at present.

Some eye diseases cannot be entirely avoided, only treated with medication or surgery as soon as recognizable symptoms appear. However, taking safety measures can often prevent or alleviate eye injury or irritation. An eye doctor should be consulted if sight changes or deteriorates, if an eye hurts, if foreign matter punctures the eye or becomes lodged in it, if an injury results in a

Living Painting *at the Museum of Modern Art in New York makes a playful comment upon the ambiguous relationship between illusion and reality by spray painting an observer's arm.*

"black eye," if chemicals enter the eye, if the eyelids stick together, if bright light bothers the eyes, or if they remain bloodshot for several days for no obvious reason.

Simple precautionary measures can guard against injury to vision: One should wear sunglasses in bright sunlight, safety goggles when using power tools, and proper eyewear during sports activities, such as face protectors for hockey or any game where the eyes risk being struck by objects or other players.

It is not true that sight can be damaged by reading too much or in poor light or by sitting too close to a television; nevertheless, these practices may tire the eyes and make them red and sore. Applying a washcloth dampened with clean, cool water can relieve this minor discomfort. It is not a good idea to use eyedrops unless a doctor advises them.

Through the sense of sight people can read, experience art, catch the expression on a friend's face, view the beauties of the earth, and look at the stars. How human beings are able to transform the physical process of seeing to actual comprehension of what they see remains to a degree unfathomable. Nevertheless, scientific research continues to increase people's understanding of the process of vision as well as to refine medicine's ability to preserve the intricate mechanism of sight, one of the most vital and pleasurable of the five ways in which humans perceive themselves and their world.

•　　　•　　　•　　　•

HEARING

"Music has charms to soothe a savage breast," wrote the English dramatist William Congreve. His words express a truth that people have known since earliest times: Sounds, musical or otherwise, have powerful effects. In Greek mythology, the Sirens' song lured sailors onto treacherous rocks, and in the Old Testament, Joshua's trumpet blast felled the walls of the city of Jericho. Today, scientists can actually measure the effect of sound on the human ear. Unhappily, much of their data point to the negative, rather than the positive, impacts of excessive noise. In London and Los Angeles, for instance, a study reported higher rates of mental illness among people who lived near noisy airports than among the general population.

One of the first scientists to record information about the sense of sound was the Greek philosopher Pythagoras, who in the 6th century B.C. made the connection between a sound's pitch and the speed of an object's vibration. For example, the low ring of a slowly clanging bell increases in pitch in proportion to the speed of its vibrations. Two hundred years later Aristotle theorized that air carried sound, and 300 years after that the Roman engineer

The 17th-century British chemist Robert Boyle (left) working with Lenin Pepin on his pneumatic machine. With this device Boyle proved that sound waves depend upon air to travel.

Vitruvius discovered that sound moves in air the way waves move in water.

However, not until the mid-1600s did the English chemist Robert Boyle demonstrate that air is essential for sound. He proved this by placing a bell inside an airtight jar. While ringing the bell, he gradually drew all the air out of the jar. As he did so, the sound grew more and more faint until, when there was no more air in the jar, the bell made no sound at all.

While these scientists were expanding man's knowledge of the physics of sound, others began to explore the anatomy and physiology of the ear. The Italian scientist Anton Maria Valsalva provided the first detailed description of the human ear in his 1704 book *On the Human Ear*. In 1777 the German scientist Philip Meckel declared that the inner ear was filled, not with air, as had been thought until then, but with fluid. He discovered this by extracting a temporal bone (the skull bone deep within which the inner-ear parts are located) from a human corpse and leaving it outside throughout a cold winter's night. In the morning he broke the bone and found the inner ear's fluid, the cochlear fluid, frozen solid inside.

Another century passed before another Italian anatomist, Alfonso Corti, discovered the ear's sensory hairs and nerve endings. However, no one understood how they worked. That discovery had to wait yet another 100 years until 1930 when scientists E. G. Wever and C. W. Bray of Princeton University found that the cochlea, a snail-shaped canal in the inner ear, behaves much like a microphone. They showed how the cochlea transforms the physical motion of the eardrum into electrical charges that can be picked up by the hairs and transmitted by the nerves.

Later still, in 1962, American scientist Georg von Békésy won the Nobel Prize in medicine for his outstanding discoveries about the anatomy and physiology of the ear. He was the first to discover how sound waves move within the inner ear and to build a model of the cochlea itself.

SOUND WAVES

Sound needs air; in fact, sound travels in air in much the same way that waves spread out in all directions from a pebble dropped into a pond. A sound wave begins when something disturbs the air. A bell, for instance, vibrates when it is struck; its vibrations make the air around it vibrate, and when the air temperature is 68 degrees Fahrenheit, the sound waves spread at the rate of 1,125 feet per second, or approximately 756 miles per hour. When the temperature drops, air molecules move more slowly, as do sound waves traveling through them; when it rises and air molecules circulate more quickly, the speed of vibrations picks up slightly.

If one were to draw a picture of a sound wave, the picture would resemble a wavy line. A loud sound has taller waves than a soft one and is said to have a higher intensity. Scientists measure a sound's intensity in watts; that is, the amount of power striking a square centimeter (.155 square inch) of a surface such as the eardrum. The loudness of the sound people hear is not exactly proportional to its intensity, however, because the human ear has a built-in, volume-lowering mechanism that protects it from being injured by very intense sound waves. Thus, doubling the intensity of a potentially dangerous sound results in only about a 23% increase in the loudness people actually hear.

Loudness itself is measured in decibels. The average human ear can hear sounds so faint that their decibel level is near zero. Normal talking is about 80 decibels, whereas sounds above 130 decibels cause pain because they are too loud for the ear to take in without doing damage to its delicate internal parts. The same-sized segment from a drawing of a high-pitched sound, such as that made by a squeaking door, has more waves in it than does that of a low-pitched sound, such as that made by a bass drum. The pitch of a sound is determined by its waves' frequency, measured in cycles per second.

Most young people can hear sounds pitched as low as 20 vibrations per second and as high as 15,000 per second, although the ability to hear high frequencies decreases with age—to 12,000 at age 50 and 6,000 by age 70. In contrast, a cat can hear sounds as high pitched as 25,000 cycles per second, a dog, 35,000, some moths react to sounds at 100,000 cycles per second, and a seal can hear sounds as high as 160,000 cycles per second. Whales make and hear sounds in a range from 50,000 to 200,000 cycles per second, so their entire hearing range consists of sounds humans cannot sense at all.

AUDITORY RECEPTION

Once a sound wave reaches the ear, it enters the auricle, the fleshy part of the ear that extends outside the head. The auricle, whose shape serves to collect sound waves, receives sound waves and directs them into the ear canal. This passageway is about an inch deep. Sound waves bounce off its walls, vibrating more quickly once inside and so becoming amplified. By the time a sound wave reaches the inner end of the canal, its volume has increased to two to four times what it was when it entered the ear.

At the inner end of the ear canal the eardrum divides the outer ear from the middle ear. The incoming sound waves make the eardrum vibrate, and the vibrating drum causes the three bones in the middle ear—the hammer, anvil, and stirrup—to vibrate in turn. For each small movement of the hammer, the stirrup moves several times, increasing the sound wave's vibration as it moves deeper into the ear. By the time the sound wave enters the inner ear, its force is 90 times what it was in the middle ear.

Muscles in the middle ear protect the ear from sudden loud sounds; some stiffen the eardrum so it doesn't vibrate as much, and others move the stirrup bone away from the inner ear. Still, because sound can move faster than muscles, sudden loud sounds are capable of breaking the eardrum or causing the stirrup to damage inner ear structures before the muscles have time to react.

Also protecting the ear is the eustachian tube, which allows excess pressure to escape through passages connecting the middle ear to the nose and mouth. However, the eustachian tube also allows infections to spread from the nose to the ear, which is why a cold sometimes leads to an ear infection.

The bones of the middle ear send vibrations through an area called the oval window, a thin skinlike membrane one-thirtieth the size of the eardrum. The oval window covers the cochlea, which is a snail-shaped structure about the size of a fingertip within the inner ear. The cochlea performs two functions: First, its semicircular canals are filled with fluid whose shifting tells the brain about the body's position, thus helping the body keep its balance. It is due to this shifting that people can tell "up" from "down" even with their eyes closed. It also accounts for the diz-

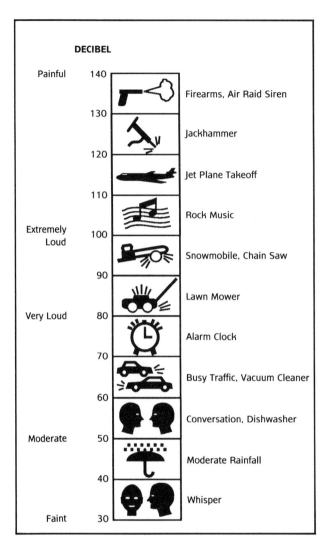

DECIBEL

Loudness	Decibel		Sound
Painful	140		Firearms, Air Raid Siren
	130		Jackhammer
	120		Jet Plane Takeoff
	110		Rock Music
Extremely Loud	100		Snowmobile, Chain Saw
	90		Lawn Mower
Very Loud	80		Alarm Clock
	70		Busy Traffic, Vacuum Cleaner
	60		Conversation, Dishwasher
Moderate	50		Moderate Rainfall
	40		Whisper
Faint	30		

This chart lists the approximate decibel level of some common noises.

ziness one feels after spinning around. The motion of fluid in the canals does not stop at once, and the canals send chaotic signals to the brain that produce the sensation of dizziness.

The second function of the cochlea is to change sound into nerve impulses. In the cochlea's vestibular and tympanic canals, the movement of the middle ear's bones forces fluid to move around the cochlear duct and over the basilar membrane and Reissner's membrane, which separate the two canals. As it moves, the fluid stimulates the organ of Corti, a small body of tissue about an inch long, containing approximately 17,000 tiny hairs. These hairs bend when stimulated by fluid moving in the cochlea. Somehow—scientists do not know precisely how—the movement of these hairs stimulates the 30,000 nerve fibers leading from the organ of Corti to its acoustic nerve.

The acoustic nerve carries the nerve impulses to the cerebral cortex, but their route is a circuitous one, as they pass through several relay stations along the way. The first one is called the cochlear nucleus. Next are the superior olive, the inferior colliculus, and, finally, the medial geniculate. At each one of these stations, the limbic system helps the brain decide which sounds to block off and which sounds to pay attention to and send to a higher level of the brain. This explains why a mother may not consciously hear normal background sounds of her child at play but will instantly respond to even a distant cry of alarm; her brain pays attention to the sound it knows is important, whereas it dismisses the rest.

The part of the cerebral cortex that processes hearing signals is called the auditory cortex, located mostly in the temporal lobes. Low-pitched sounds are sent to outer areas of the cortex, whereas high-pitched sounds are processed in deeper ones. But other areas help the brain know what has been heard: A bit to the rear of the auditory cortex lies a memory area where sound memories are stored. If the area is destroyed by injury or disease, a person will still be able to hear, but will not recognize the meaning of the sounds.

Two ears are necessary to locate sounds. For instance, the brain gauges the location of a growling dog by comparing the speed at which the sound arrives at each ear. Although the ear closest to the growl will receive the sound only a few millionths of a second before the other ear, this provides sufficient information for the brain to determine the location of the sound. Biaural, or two-eared, hearing also allows people to hear one sound with one ear and a second one with the other. But when the sounds consist of speech, the brain can understand only one message at a time because the brain is equipped to process only one at a time. This is why, when listening to someone while talking on the telephone, people cannot readily take in what the person next to them is saying.

Gallaudet University: Making the Hearing World Listen

Society has consistently equated deafness with a lack of intelligence. Aristotle said that those "born deaf become senseless and incapable of reason." In ancient Greece deaf babies were left out in the countryside to die; in the Middle Ages the deaf were barred from worship in churches and were not allowed to marry or own property. Not until the 16th century did a few clergymen begin to teach the deaf.

By the 19th century, deaf people had founded 22 schools in the United States. In 1864, Edward Miner Gallaudet founded Gallaudet University in Washington, D.C., and in that same year President Abraham Lincoln authorized it to confer college degrees. For more than a century, Gallaudet has remained the only liberal arts college for the deaf in the world. Aside from teaching its students to use American Sign Language (ASL), read lips, speak, and in other ways compensate for their disability, Gallaudet offers an education similar to that of many American colleges.

Its 2,500 students select undergraduate and graduate courses within the schools of Communication, Education and Human Services, Management, and Arts and Sciences. They participate in sports, give theatrical performances, and dance to music—music so loud it shakes the floors of the student union social room. "I love music," says senior David Connor, who experiences the music by feeling its vibrations. "Practice," he says, "and in time you get not only the vibration but the feel of the emotions, too."

Gallaudet serves another important function as well—that of helping young people develop a sense of belonging both to the international community of deaf people and to the hearing world. Many students worry about getting a job after they graduate. Says Irvine Stewart, "I'm scared to go out in the hearing world. There are so many things I can do, but

Students in a classroom at Gallaudet University.

so many limits imposed [by hearing people] on how I can do them. I'm talking about really making it." But says Jenny Israel, another Gallaudet student, "All I have to do is impress [a job interviewer] with myself. I will speak for myself, interact with the interviewer, and show that I am motivated to do the job."

In addition to the usual joys and pressures any college student faces, Gallaudet students also confront controversy arising from the gap between the deaf world and that of the hearing. In March 1988, when a hearing woman was appointed president of the university over the popular and highly qualified deaf candidate, I. King Jordan, the conflict between the two worlds came to a head. The campus erupted in an angry protest that led to a week of marches and speechmaking by students and faculty alike. Before long, the issue caught the public's eye, making headline news and gaining support from congressmen and even Vice-president George Bush.

The organized voice of protest toppled the opposition, and Jordan became the first deaf president of Gallaudet. With his victory came tremendous challenge. Beyond making decisions about the educational life of Gallaudet's campus, its curriculum, and staff, Jordan travels throughout the country speaking on behalf of the deaf community and lobbies on Capitol Hill for the disabled. However diverse his responsibilities, Jordan claims a single goal: to bridge the gap between the hearing world and that of the deaf by educating people to understand each other's needs. "The only thing deaf people can't do," Jordan tirelessly repeats, "is hear."

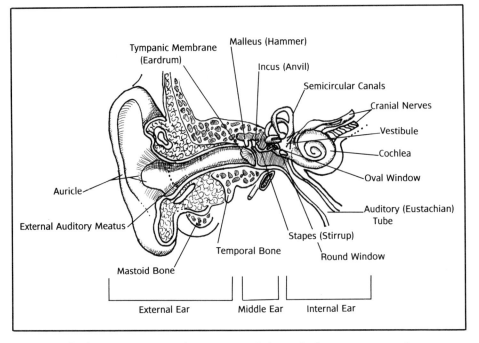

The human ear. Sound waves travel through the outer ear to the ear-drum, whose vibrations set the middle ear bones into motion. The bones stir the cochlea's fluid, which stimulates auditory nerve endings to carry nerve impulses to the hearing area in the cerebral cortex.

HEARING IMPAIRMENTS

About 200,000 Americans are deaf, and another 3 million have severe hearing problems. Hearing difficulties are of two kinds: conduction hearing loss, in which the outer or middle ear does not transmit sound properly; and sensory-neural hearing loss, or nerve deafness, in which the problem lies either in the inner ear's organ of Corti, the acoustic nerve, or in the auditory cortex of the brain.

The most common problem of the outer ear is the buildup of excessive cerumen, or earwax, in the ear canal. Glands in the ear canal produce this wax as a way of trapping dirt or foreign objects and keeping them from getting into the middle ear, but if too much wax builds up, it blocks the ear from receiving sound. Excessive wax should be removed by a doctor because digging around in one's own ear with a cotton swab or other instrument can cause serious damage.

More severe damage can occur if a sudden, very loud sound, such as an explosion, injures or even ruptures the eardrum; such a sound can cause permanent hearing loss or complete deafness. Middle-ear infections are painful and in severe cases may also damage or rupture the eardrum or even infect the bone behind the ear, the mastoid bone. Once potentially fatal, this latter complication is now treatable with antibiotics or, when necessary, with surgery.

Otosclerosis is a condition in which there is an abnormal growth of tissue around the bones of the middle ear. The tissue hardens, stopping the bones from moving properly. The only treatment for this middle-ear disease, which is thought to be genetically transmitted, used to be a drastic surgical procedure called fenestration (opening a window between the middle and inner ear). Today, microsurgery (surgery performed with the aid of a miscroscope) offers a safer corrective procedure for freeing the middle ear's tiny bones from the abnormal tissue that traps them.

High-decibel sound or prolonged exposure to sound can cause problems of the inner ear. The decibel level at a rock concert is often as high as 130 decibels, and some home stereo equipment can produce sound at more than 140 decibels. Ears can be damaged from 2 or 3 hours of exposure to only 90 decibels, whereas repeated exposure increases the risk of hearing loss by destroying the tiny hair cells on the organ of Corti.

The inner ear inflammation called labyrinthitis causes pain, dizziness, and acute nausea. If not treated with antibiotics, permanent and complete deafness may result. Tumors of the inner ear, called acoustic neuromas, can also result in deafness. Often genetically inherited, these tumors are benign and do not spread to other areas of the body, but if untreated they can nonetheless prove fatal because they grow large enough to press on vital brain structures. However, if acoustic neuromas are diagnosed early enough, they can be surgically removed.

The National Institute of Neurological and Communicative Disorders has found tinnitus, a ringing in the ears, to be the most common complaint of patients with ear trouble. For some it is curable; for others, neither a cause nor a cure can be found. In some cases, the patient may be experiencing an adverse reaction to a medication. Many drugs, ranging from antibiotics to simple aspirin, can cause temporary or permanent hearing loss. If this occurs, doctors should either reduce the dosage or substitute another medication.

Another recognizable cause of tinnitus is Ménière's disease, which occurs when there is too much fluid in the inner-ear canals. This results in increased pressure within the canals, causing them to swell. Ringing in the ears is accompanied by nausea, vomiting, dizziness, and hearing loss in one or both ears. There is no single reliable treatment for Ménière's disease, but sometimes symptoms are relieved when patients avoid coffee, tobacco, and alcohol. Others need drugs or surgery to reduce the swelling, and in some cases the attacks resist all treatment. The origin of Ménière's disease remains unknown.

Modern surgical procedures are often able to correct hearing problems. Bone or nerve transplants can replace damaged ear parts, for instance. And many other types of impaired hearing can be improved with hearing aids, battery-powered devices that pick up sound, amplify it, and direct it into the ear. The electronic inner parts of today's hearing aids are so small that they are put together under a microscope, and the aids themselves are practically undetectable to all but the wearer.

However, hearing aids cannot alleviate all hearing disabilities; some are good for certain problems, some for others. A patient who wants a hearing aid should go first to a physician, who can help him or her determine which device to buy; then to a hearing-aid dealer; and finally to an audiologist, a hearing specialist, who will instruct the patient in the use of his or her aid.

Deafness and Communication

A person born deaf encounters special difficulties in learning to communicate. A deaf baby will never speak without special training, because people generally learn to speak by imitating sounds that they hear. At age 2, even with special help, a deaf child can recognize only about 50 words compared to the 1,500 known by the child who can hear.

If no one realizes that a child is deaf, his or her speech and other related problems may be thought to indicate mental retardation. In the past, some deaf people were even thought to be

Although Helen Keller (left) was blind and deaf since infancy, her teacher Anne Sullivan (right) helped her learn Braille and recognize speech by "hearing" vibrations on the speaker's larynx.

insane and were sent to mental institutions. Even today, the deaf are sometimes ignored or avoided or treated as if they lack intelligence. This can be terribly painful, especially for young adults who want to be like their schoolmates, to have friends and be treated the same way everyone else is. Instead, deaf people often suffer from intense loneliness, sometimes compounded by ridicule from their peers.

This emotional pain can be prevented if the hearing treat the deaf the same way they treat everyone else. At the same time, though, some of the deaf need special attention so that they can learn to communicate and be effective in daily life. Special schools teach deaf children to communicate both by speech and by sign language, hand signals that allow them to express their needs, thoughts, and feelings. In these schools, deaf children are also taught to read lips so that they can learn to understand spoken words by watching the movement of the speaker's mouth.

One college for the deaf, Gallaudet University, has recently made great strides not only in educating deaf young adults and preparing them for careers but in helping them to realize that they are just as good, smart, and able to contribute to society as people who can hear. Furthermore, a host of devices is now available, such as telephones that type messages for those who cannot hear, which enable deaf people to live a normal life.

• • • •

CHAPTER 4

SMELL

The English Girl *by Childe Hassam*

The sense of smell is the one that most powerfully provokes memories and feelings. The smell of rubbing alcohol is a reminder of the doctor's office; the aroma of buttered popcorn brings the movies readily to mind. For the French author Marcel Proust, the smell of tea and cake stirred up the powerful memory that engendered his multivolume literary work, *Remembrance of Things Past*. The sense of smell may serve as a warning, such as in the smell of smoke, or as an attraction, as in the aroma of dinner cooking. It is also responsible for about 75% of what is commonly referred to as taste; pepper and cheese, for instance, can hardly be tasted by people who lack the sense of smell.

AN ANCIENT SENSE

The sense of smell is linked to memories and feelings, as well as to the sense of taste, because of the way the anatomy of smelling has evolved. Millions of years ago, early sea animals had primitive brains consisting of a small lump of nerve cells connected to smell-taste sensors on their outer bodies. These sensors detected traces of chemicals in the water around them, thereby helping them to locate food, notice enemies, and find mates.

At first, the nerve-tissue lumps were used only for processing, recognizing, and remembering smell information and for primitive emotions about the smells, such as fear when an enemy was sensed or pleasure when food was eaten. As animals evolved, some of them became land dwellers. These land dwellers needed to sense chemicals, not in water, but in the air. Thus in land-dwelling creatures, the sense of smell divided from the sense of taste. Meanwhile, in both water and land creatures, the nerve tissue became more complex; over millions of years, the modern brain developed from the prehistoric lump of nerve cells originally devoted to the sense of smell.

Some primitive structures remain intact within the human brain. Buried deep inside, they form the limbic system, a group of structures located in the brain's temporal lobes and near the thalamus. Among these structures are the amygdala, which regulates emotions, particularly that of anger; the septum pellucidum, which controls pleasurable sensations; and the hippocampus, which processes emotions and memories and regulates how much attention one pays to sensory signals. It is likely that smells evoke feelings and memories with such power because the sense of smell is the earliest to have evolved. Another reason may be that, unlike the other senses, smell signals travel to the limbic system without being processed first by the thalamus.

THE APPARATUS OF SMELL

Although scientists are not yet able to explain fully how smells trigger emotion and memory, they do know that the sense of smell is stimulated when the nose breathes in the molecules that substances called volatiles give off into the air. Volatile substances have a stronger smell when warm than when cold because heat causes more molecules to separate from them and float into the air. Air carrying these volatile molecules first enters the nose through the nasal cavities (the two holes at the end of the nose) and the mouth. From there, only about 2% of the inhaled air moves to the olfactory epithelium (or "smelling skin") in the upper part of the very rear of the nasal cavities behind and just above the bridge of the nose. But because of the sensitive nature of the human smelling apparatus, this small percentage is sufficient.

The olfactory epithelium consists of two tiny patches whose area totals about one square inch. Between the cells are special chemoreceptors, or cells that react to chemical substances. The thousands of epithelial cells and the chemoreceptors are covered with a thin coat of mucus, a sticky fluid. Tiny hairs called cilia grow from the ends of the chemoreceptors and extend into the fluid; each cilium is from four to eight hundred-thousandths of an inch long. When molecules of a substance dissolve in the fluid and touch a chemoreceptor's cilia, the cell reacts.

Scientists do not know how many different kinds of chemoreceptors there are in the olfactory epithelium or what makes things smell the way they do. They have made attempts, though, to divide all smells into a few categories: One such classification assigns all smells to the category of floral, camphorous (like mothballs), musky (like skunk), minty, etherlike (like nail polish), pungent (like lemon), or putrid (like rotten eggs). But these are fairly arbitrary classifications; no system has been found that neatly labels every possible kind of smell.

In addition, scientists do not know what it is about a molecule—possibly its size, its shape, or the electrical charge it carries—that causes smell chemoreceptors to react to it or what allows receptors to distinguish among different smells. A person with a good sense of smell can notice 10,000 different odors, yet it seems unlikely that there is 1 kind of chemoreceptor for each possible smell distinguished by the nose, whose total number is about 20 million. That people can distinguish new, artificially made smells supports this supposition; it is hard to imagine how the nose could develop special chemoreceptors in anticipation

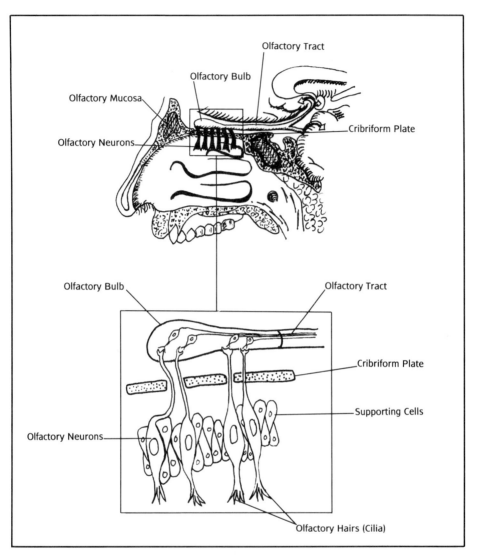

A cross section of the nasal cavity shows the olfactory bulb. Once smells have been processed within the bulb they travel through the olfactory tract to the cerebral cortex.

of such smells. It is more likely that only a few kinds of chemoreceptors produce different smells and that these chemoreceptors are in turn triggered in different numbers and combinations by different kinds of molecules.

A further unsolved mystery about the sense of smell has to do

A further unsolved mystery about the sense of smell has to do with precisely what reaction occurs in the stimulated chemoreceptor to produce a nerve impulse that can travel to the brain. But however this process takes place, a nerve impulse is produced, which then travels up the body of the chemoreceptor from its outer hairlike endings to its inner nerve fibers. These fibers run through holes in the ethmoid (the bony ceiling at the rear of the nose) to the cranial cavity, which holds the brain. Upon their exit from the nasal cavity, nerve fibers bundle together into structures called olfactory bulbs; at this point a person knows he or she has smelled something but is unable to identify it. Next, the impulses travel through the first cranial nerve to the brain's olfactory cortex deep within the limbic system. This is where the smell is identified.

The nerve signals then go to different areas in the brain, the thalamus and cerebral cortex, where the smell integrates with other sensory experience and with knowledge. For instance, the smell of fish cooking means someone is having fish for dinner; eating fish is good for people. The signals also travel to the hippocampus and amygdala of the limbic system, areas that give rise to feelings and memories. For one person, for example, the smell of fish may bring up the memory of a summer vacation at the shore and may also be associated with a feeling of loneliness because that summer he or she felt lonely.

Nerve fibers carrying signals from the sense of smell also reach the hypothalamus, where the body's appetite centers are. This is why the smell of food cooking can make people hungry, and it is also the reason food becomes unappetizing if a person has a cold and cannot smell it.

In addition, because it is entwined with the limbic system, which controls our most basic feelings, the sense of smell may well play a role in evoking emotions related to sexual attraction. Although scientists have been able to verify that people do like to approach objects—and other people—that smell good, researchers have not yet arrived at a detailed description of how and why the sense of smell contributes to human beings' reproductive activity.

This connection between sexual attraction and the sense of smell is not as important for humans as it is for animals. For instance, hamsters that cannot smell their mates lose all interest in them, whereas, according to Robert Henkin, of the Center for

Sensory Disorders at Georgetown University, only one in four people who lose their sense of smell lose some, if not all, interest in sexual activity.

The chemicals in smells affecting animals' reproductive behavior are called pheromones, and some scientists think they have an effect upon the behavior of humans as well. In 1970 the psychologist Martha McClintock of the University of Chicago's Department of Behavioral Sciences noted that the menstrual cycles of women who live together tend to become synchronized. A 1988 study by George Preti and Winnifred Cutler of the University of Pennsylvania and the Monell Chemical Senses Center supplied information about how this adjustment actually occurs. For a period of 3 months, every few days they exposed 10 women to the smell of underarm perspiration from other women. At the end of the three months, the menstrual cycles of women assigned the task of smelling the donated sweat had adjusted so that they coincided with the cycles of those whose perspiration they smelled. Apparently a pheromone in the perspiration adjusted the biological rhythms of those women who smelled it.

But such apparently automatic responses to some smells are not the only kind of response to odors. What people know or have been trained to think contributes to the way they experience a smell. People in American society, for instance, think of perspiration as unpleasant; it therefore tends to summon up negative images of uncleanliness. It is true that it is better to wash than to be dirty, because cleanliness is a means of disease prevention. But attitudes toward body odors also come from advertising, which influences the public to think body smells are unpleasant so that people will buy soap, perfume, and deodorants.

Memory, too, affects whether one perceives smells as pleasant or unpleasant. If a person knows that the smell of soup is always followed by a delicious meal, for instance, he or she will tend to like the soup smell. But if the smell is usually followed by an electric shock, the person will soon grow to dislike the smell itself.

ANOSMIA

About 2 million Americans cannot smell anything at all. They suffer from anosmia, the inability to smell or taste. One-quarter of the population between the ages of 65 and 80 have some degree

A demonstration of response to a hazardous waste emergency. Exposure to toxic waste may destroy any part of the sensory system.

of anosmia, and almost half of those over 80 have it. Although no one knows why elderly people lose their sense of smell, this may explain why people's appetites tend to grow smaller with age. Head injury is the most common cause of anosmia among young people; about 1 in 15 victims of serious head trauma loses his or her sense of taste and smell, many of them permanently.

Anosmia can also be inherited or result from allergy, infection, exposure to toxic chemicals, or a brain tumor, or it may be caused by no apparent reason at all. People who cannot smell or taste are in danger from fires whose smoke they cannot detect, from gas leaks, and from spoiled food; moreover, they cannot enjoy any of the smells or tastes most people take for granted. Medication can help certain types of anosmia by reducing inflammation of nerves; the condition may also respond to allergy treatments or to surgery. But for many sufferers there is as yet no cure.

.   .   .   .

CHAPTER 5

TASTE

In 1895 a nine-year-old boy named Tom saw a cup he thought contained a cold drink, grabbed it, and took a huge gulp before realizing his mistake: The cup held boiling-hot chowder instead. The hot soup severely burned his esophagus, the tube through which food travels into the stomach, and the scar from this burn closed the esophagus permanently. Doctors inserted an artificial tube through his abdomen directly into his stomach so he would not starve, but Tom lost weight anyway and always felt hungry

Benedetto Gennari's portrait of the Italian physician Marcello Malpighi, who discovered taste buds. Malpighi holds his influential book on the anatomy of plants, Anatomes Plantarum Idea.

no matter what kind of food was poured into the tube. Finally he told the doctors he thought he would feel better if he could taste his food; from then on he put a bit of it into his mouth— even though he could not swallow it—before pouring the rest directly into his stomach. Once he began doing so, Tom gained weight and lost his constant hungry feeling.

Why tasting made Tom thrive, however, was a mystery to his doctors, and even now the sense of taste is one of the least understood of the senses. The taste buds were completely unknown until the Italian anatomist Marcello Malpighi discovered them in the 17th century. And it was not until the 1800s that the German scientists Georg Meissner and Rudolf Wagner first described taste cells, the cells within the taste buds, after viewing them through a microscope. Precisely how these cells work is unknown even today, and the question of why things taste the way they do—what it is in lemon juice that makes it taste sour, for example—is still a subject of energetic study and debate.

What is known is that when people enjoy the taste of their meals, their digestive system works better. In one study by Drs. Henry Janowitz and Franklin Hollander of Mt. Sinai Hospital in New York City, people who chose nutritious foods that tasted good produced twice as much digestive juice as did people who ate a tasteless but nutritious meal. The digestive juices of the people who chose tasty food also flowed two times faster and for twice as long as did the digestive juices of people given bland food.

In short, the taste of food is not just a pleasant side effect of getting nutrition. Taste itself is important to the way the body receives nutrients from the food it digests. The sense of taste also helps protect people from illness or injury. It is immediately evident from a tiny taste whether food is spoiled or if it tastes rotten, moldy, or sour; the bad taste of poison is often easily detected as well. The pleasure a person experiences when eating is important to survival because the desire for food serves as a stimulus to eat, a process essential to life itself. The importance of tasting has even found its way into everyday language in that a curious person may be said to have "a taste for learning," whereas one who likes excitement has "a taste for adventure."

THE MECHANICS OF TASTE

Tasting begins on the tongue, a muscular organ located inside the mouth. The tongue is attached by skin and muscle on its lower side to the floor of the mouth and at the rear to a small bone, the hyoid bone, lodged in the tongue's muscle tissue. The skin on the top surface of the tongue contains about 10,000 tiny chemical-sensing bodies called taste buds. These organs are located in the tongue's visible bumps, called papillae, which give the tongue its spongy-looking surface and which occur in four shapes: filiform (pointed), foliate (leaf shaped), fungiform (mushroom shaped), and circumvallate (ring shaped). Each foliate, fungiform, and circumvallate papilla holds 1 to 200 taste buds. Although filiform papillae are the most numerous type, they contain no taste buds.

Inside a single taste bud are about a dozen taste cells, each about four-thousandths of an inch long and half that thick. A few taste cells in each taste bud have tiny taste hairs sticking out of the bud through an opening called a taste pore. The hairs are bathed in saliva, the fluid produced by the salivary glands on the sides and lower surface of the tongue.

Saliva helps the body use food in three ways. Chewing mixes the food and moistens it with saliva so it can be swallowed more easily. Saliva also contains an enzyme, or chemical, that helps break starch molecules, such as those found in bread, into forms the body can use. Molecules of food also dissolve in saliva, so they become small enough to flow into contact with taste hairs poking out of the taste buds.

The taste buds can sense four main categories of taste: sweet, sour, bitter, and salt. The tip of the tongue senses sweet tastes most strongly, and the sides are more sensitive to sour ones. Bitter tastes are detected mostly at the back of the tongue, and salt can be tasted most strongly at the front, although salt is detectable to some degree on most areas of the tongue's top surface. There is no clear line dividing these areas, and the taste buds themselves do not all specialize in sensing just one sort of taste. Some taste cells react only to salt, for example, but others can sense more than one kind of taste or even all four of them.

Just what makes things taste the way they do is not yet known. Something about a molecule of sugar makes it taste sweet, but no one is sure what. Scientists have tried to categorize tastes by molecule size and shape, by weight, by the kind of electrical charge the molecule may carry, and by many other character-istics, but they have not yet found a rule to explain what attributes a molecule must possess to make it taste a certain way.

Nor is it known what happens when a molecule touches a taste hair that makes the taste cell react to it. Somehow, though, the meeting of molecule and taste hair causes a reaction within the taste cell, and this reaction—again, scientists do not know pre-cisely how—stimulates a complex network of nerve fibers at the cell's root. Perhaps because of the mingling of these nerve fibers, tastes are able to affect one another. Salt, for example, brings out the flavor of some meats and soups. This principle has been adapted to form an accepted part of the daily routine in the

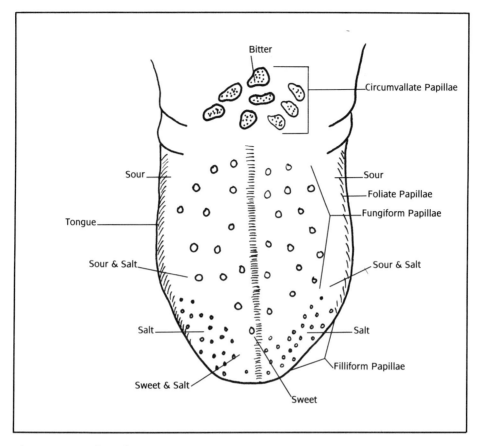

The tongue with its four shapes of papillae and four main categories of taste buds: sweet, sour, bitter, and salt. The thousands of tiny papillae give the tongue its finely corrugated look and feel.

African country of Ghana, where it is customary to eat bits of a plant called *syncipalium mirabilis* in the morning because it makes food eaten during the rest of the day taste sweeter.

From nerves at the root of the taste cells, taste impulses travel to two principle nerves, called the lingual nerve and the chorda tympani; they also carry sensations of temperature, touch, and pain from the tongue. The sensations travel along the main nerves to the medulla, at the very top of the spinal cord, in an area known as the brain stem. From there, the impulses travel to the thalamus, the brain's central relay station for information from all the senses, except that of smell.

The Role of the Sense of Smell

The thalamus forwards the taste information to a part of the cerebral cortex, the brain's outer layer, where taste sensations are recognized and experienced. Meanwhile it relays touch, temperature, and pain signals, if there are any, to areas in the cortex that specialize in their processing. And at the same time, information from the sense of smell, which is active before and during eating, travels through the limbic system to the cortex.

The sense of smell contributes tremendously to the experience of taste, partly because it is by far the more sensitive of the two senses. It takes about 25,000 times more of a substance to activate the sense of taste than it does to trigger the sense of smell. The influence of smell upon taste is demonstrated when a person has a cold, for when the nose is stuffed up and unable to smell food, the person has trouble tasting food as well. By a method scientists still do not understand, the brain mingles these two different sensations into the unified experience of taste.

The brain also makes judgments about this experience, deciding whether or not the food tastes good or bad. To some degree, these judgments are based on what a person knows and what he or she is used to eating. In lands where insects are a normal part of the diet, for instance, people enjoy eating them, whereas they might think a cheeseburger, to them a strange kind of food, tastes disgusting.

The Brain and the Hypothalamus

It is also true, however, that people tend to like the taste of things that contain substances their body needs. Babies who have a deficiency of vitamin D seem to enjoy the strong fishy taste of cod-liver oil, whereas most people find its taste quite unpleasant. The body's need for especially large amounts of this vitamin during early growth apparently causes the brain to "like" the oil.

A lack of some substances may even cause people to crave their taste; salt is one of these. Salt helps the body keep the proper amount of water in its tissues. When the body has too little salt, as, for example, in a hot climate where excessive perspiration makes it lose more salt than usual, people tend to want more salt on their food. Too high a salt level in the body causes thirst;

this is why eating salty snacks leads to a craving for beverages. Both reactions are triggered by the area of the brain called the hypothalamus.

Located just below the thalamus, this small, plum-shaped part of the brain contains the body's hunger and thirst centers. Triggered by too much or too little salt, by high or low levels of sugars in the blood, and by signals from an empty or full stomach, as well as by many other complex chemicals and functions, the hypothalamus not only stimulates people to eat food or drink, but by influencing the way the cerebral cortex processes these sensations, it also actually alters the taste, smell, and appearance of food. This is why a sandwich may not be particularly appealing to a person who is not hungry, but it may look, smell, and taste delicious to a person who is. This is also why a person who is desperately thirsty may think a drink of plain water is the best-tasting thing in the world.

In cooperation with the emotion-regulating limbic system, the hypothalamus also produces feelings about food, drink, and their tastes. This is the reason, for example, an accidental gulp of sour milk causes not only an unpleasant physical sensation but also a feeling of emotional disgust. Positive feelings about food also

Peter Kranz, a science teacher, shows his students how to enjoy sautéed cicadas. Familiarity is one of the many ways in which the brain determines its likes and dislikes.

come from the hypothalamus, especially from the part of the limbic system called the septum pellucidum, one of the brain's "pleasure centers." It is in these areas that much of the enjoyment people derive from food originates.

LOSS OF TASTE

Taste tends to become less sensitive as people age because, after age 45, some taste cells die and are not replaced. A simple cold can also temporarily keep people from tasting food, mostly because they cannot smell it. And, at any age, injury to the brain, nerves, or tongue can cause the permanent loss of taste and smelling abilities called anosmia, which was discussed in the preceding chapter.

A desire to eat nonfood substances such as ice, paint chips, laundry starch, or clay is called pica. In some, this disturbance results from lack of a substance in the diet or from the body's inability to process a substance. Children who have a calcium deficiency, a lack of the mineral needed for strong bones and teeth, may develop the habit of eating chalk or plaster, which contain calcium. In others, it may simply be a habit learned from a family member; people who eat ice or laundry starch often say they do it because a parent did it. Some of the nonfood items people eat are not harmful, but others do harm to the digestive system, so anyone who has such a habit should ask a doctor about its health effects.

•   •   •   •

CHAPTER 6

. . . .

TOUCH

The Fortune Teller *by Caravaggio*

The sense of touch provides a constant array of information about the world. Through it people can gauge the softness of a pillow, test the ripeness of a peach, or check the temperature of a sick child's forehead. Touching can be a way of communicating: a loving caress, an encouraging pat on the back, an angry slap, or a remindful tap on the shoulder. Touches warn of danger, too, by identifying hot, cold, or sharp objects or an excessive amount of pressure.

Unlike the other senses such as sight and hearing, whose receptors are confined to the relatively small, specialized organs of the eyes and ears, the sense of touch is diffused throughout the body. Its messages travel through nerve endings in the skin and are transmitted to the brain by the nervous system. The skin's nerve endings are sensitive to a variety of input—temperature, vibration, pressure, and pain—all sensations experienced through touch.

Touch is among the most recent of the senses to become an object of scientific inquiry; it was not until the mid-19th century that it began to interest researchers. German scientists Magnus Blix and Johannes Goldscheider were the first to describe, in 1884, how areas of the skin responded to pressure, cold, heat, and pain. In 1863 another German, Wilhelm Kühne (whose subsequent experimentation on the retina was referred to in Chapter 2) explained touch sensations inside the body by describing touch receptors in muscles, and in 1892 Angelo Ruffini identified the nerve endings of these receptors. During this same era other scientists used microscopes to find some of the tiny structures responsible for touch sensations. This chapter will provide a discussion of these structures in detail, along with an examination of the skin that contains them.

THE PHYSIOLOGY OF SKIN

The skin itself is an organ of the body, even though it is rarely thought of as such. If this organ could be removed and measured, the entire human skin would be about a tenth of an inch thick, weighing about 10 pounds and measuring (if spread out flat) about 20 square feet. Each square inch of skin contains 20 million cells, 95 oil glands, 650 sweat glands, and about 65 hairs, all nourished by about 15 feet of blood vessels.

The skin consists of three main layers. The outer layer, or epidermis, is about as thick as a piece of notebook paper. The innermost part of the epidermis contains color-producing cells called melanocytes, which give a person's skin its hue. Naturally dark skin has more melanocytes than light skin, whereas a suntan occurs when the sun stimulates melanocytes to produce melanin, a coloring material. The middle layer of skin is the dermis. It is stretchy because it contains fibers of elastin and collagen that allow it to snap back into shape after being stretched. The in-

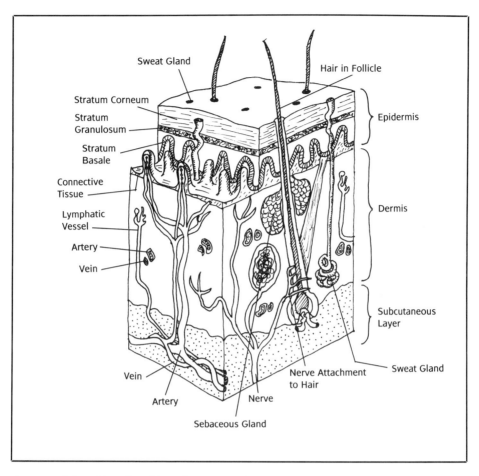

Layers of the skin. The skin's three main functions are protection, temperature control (through perspiration), and perception (as of pain, heat, and cold).

nermost layer of skin, the subcutis, is a fatty layer that both cushions the body and stores fat to use as energy in case a time should come when the body cannot get sufficient food.

The epidermis and dermis contain the nerves responsible for the sense of touch. Scientists have not yet completely identified all the different kinds of touch receptors responsible for sensing different kinds of touches. In general, however, the receptors are of two types: "capsule-type" structures that have nerve tissue inside them and "free endings," uncovered nerve ends that form complex lacy networks by winding around other cells like strings.

The capsule-type nerve ends, about which the most is known, are the Pacinian corpuscles (discovered in the mid-19th century by Italian scientist Filippo Pacini). These capsules are most numerous in the fingertips; each finger possesses as many as 100 of them. Inside these capsules are layers of cells and fluid with nerve cells at the center. Pacinian corpuscles are sensitive to pressure and vibration, and their nerve cells, the fastest reacting in the body, can respond to a pressure that dents the skin only two ten-thousandths of an inch in one-fifth of a thousandth of a second.

Another type of capsule nerve end is called Meissner's corpuscle (named for the German scientist Georg Meissner). These egg-shaped capsules are found in the skin of the fingertips, especially in the ridges of the fingerprint, and the palms, toes, lips, tongue, and genitals. They are responsible for the heightened sensitivity in these areas, and because of them a person is able to know precisely where he or she has been touched. A Meissner's corpuscle is so accurate in detecting where a touch is located that it can discern a difference of as little as eight-thousandths of an inch.

Two other kinds of capsule sensors are the end bulbs of Krause (after Wilhelm Krause) and the Ruffini corpuscles (after Angelo Ruffini). These are thought to be responsible for sensing heat or

Human skin (× 20). The dark upper border constitutes the epidermis; the wide interior section dominated by globular arteries, veins, and glands is the dermis; and the hypodermis is the more sparsely filled narrow section at the base of the photograph.

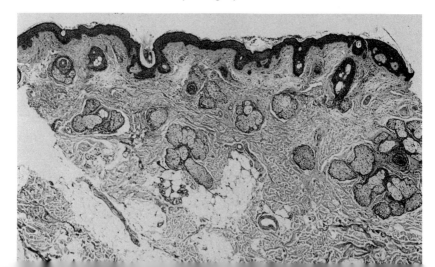

cold on the skin. But scientists do not yet understand fully just how the skin senses temperature.

The largest number of free-ending touch receptors is in the skin around hair roots, but they are also located in nonhairy skin all over the body. These exposed strands of nerve fiber sense both pressure and pain. Some free endings are so sensitive they can detect a movement of as little as four hundred-thousandths of an inch.

Scientists' main question about the sense of touch is whether each kind of touch has its own kind of capsule or free ending— a special kind of receptor for pressure, another kind for heat, still another for pain, and so on—or if just a few kinds of nerve endings can send many different kinds of touch messages to the brain.

TOUCH PATHWAYS

Nerve fibers transmit sensory impulses along pathways up the spinal cord to the brain. The pathways that ascend from the sensation to the brain are ascending, or afferent, pathways, and those that descend from the brain are efferent pathways (these control motor functions).

There are two major ascending pathways involved in conscious perception: the spinothalamic system ("spino" designates its origin in the spinal cord and "thalamic" its destination in the thalamus) and the medial lemniscal system. Other pathways carry sensations of which people are not consciously aware, such as those of balance and visual reflexes. Among these are the spinocerebellar, spinothecal, and spinorebicular systems.

The two systems are then further divided into tracts. The spinothalamic system is composed of the anterior tract, which transmits nerve impulses for light touch, pressure, tickle, and itch sensations; and its lateral tract, which transmits pain and temperature. Through the medial lemniscal system travel sensations of proprioception (perception of position), fine touch, pressure, and vibration. This system's separation into two tracts is based upon whether the source of the stimulus is located above or below the midthorax (chest area). The sensations stimulated from below travel up the fasciculus gracilis; those stimulated from above the chest pass through the fasciculus cuneatus tract.

The nerves that carry information from the skin to the spinal cord are called spinal nerves. Each pair of spinal nerves carries signals from a particular area of skin, called a dermatome. Nerve fibers carrying touch signals cross to the opposite side of the spinal cord at its base: Fibers from the body's left side go into the right side of the brain and vice versa.

Next, touch signals travel to the thalamus, the brain's first relay station for information from all the senses. The thalamus routes signals from the sense of touch to the part of the cerebral cortex responsible for processing touch information. This area recognizes, decodes, and sorts the nerve signals.

The brain must also decide whether or not to pay attention to the touch. It does this with the help of a structure in the limbic system, the hippocampus, which constantly compares sense input with what it has experienced before. If it experiences a constant unchanging pressure, the limbic system sends an "ignore it" message; this is why people are not constantly aware of such things as the pressure of shoes on their feet. But with a change in the signal, such as the sensation of a nail through the sole of the shoe, the hippocampus stops its "ignore it" message, and the cerebral cortex becomes instantly alert to the new sensation.

Touches inside the body are called somatic, which means they pertain to the body's inner walls, organs, and structure. Some inner parts of the body are designed to be sensitive to touch; people can feel their muscles moving, for instance, when they want to locate or control them. The digestive system is also capable of sensing touch, such as the feeling of pressure from a too-large meal. But other body parts are entirely insensitive to touch or to pain. Many parts of the brain, for instance, can undergo surgery without painkilling medicines because they have no touch or pain nerves. The brain-surgery patient requires anesthesia for incisions of the skin, bone, and coverings of the brain because these areas do contain pain nerves. But once the skull has been fully opened and the brain exposed, manipulation and cutting on the brain itself causes no pain whatsoever.

Feeling Pain

Pain itself is a special kind of sensory message that areas sensitive to touch often transmit. Not only the skin but other sensory organs, such as the eyes and ears, can react with pain if their

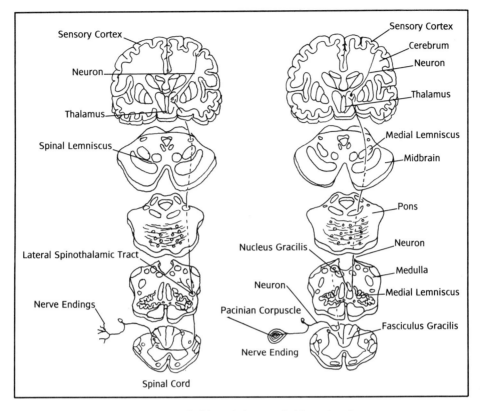

The lateral spinothalamic tract (left) and the medial lemniscal tract (right). Nerve impulses carry information up sensory pathways in the spinal cord; each ascending tract delivers a specific type of touch sensation to the thalamus, where it is transformed into sensory experience.

nerves are overloaded by a too-bright light or a too-loud sound. Scientists do not know for certain whether special pain nerves send the pain messages or if the distress signals move along nerves ordinarily used for normal sensory input. But whatever their route, pain messages begin when tissue in the body is damaged or threatened with injury.

From its infliction to its recognition, pain goes through three general stages. First, nociception occurs when nerve endings react to injury, such as burns, cuts, or sharp blows. In an instant, nerves in the damaged area signal their distress. Next, cells in the area give off chemicals to boost the pain nerves' signals; these chemicals include prostaglandin, substance P, and bradykinin, which also cause redness, swelling, and heat in the injured area. Meanwhile the nerve fibers carry the signals to two relay stations in the brain. The reticular formation in the brain stem receives the signals and sends them to the thalamus, which relays them to the cerebral cortex, where the pain is recognized and felt. In the third stage, signals move to the limbic system, which triggers feelings about the pain, such as sadness, anger, or anxiety.

TOUCH DISORDERS

Disorders of the sense of touch may result from illness or injury to the skin, nerves, or brain or to any organ that contains nerves to transmit touch signals. A troublesome—but usually minor— kind of touch disorder that afflicts many people is itching, an irritation of the skin that causes intense discomfort and the desire to scratch. Its causes include insect bites, athlete's foot (a fungus infection of the skin), allergies, and some whole-body ailments like chicken pox and measles. Itching may also occur as a side effect of some medicines, or it may even be symptomatic of a serious illness such as Hodgkin's disease, a type of cancer. Thus, although one can ignore harmless itching or soothe it with calamine lotion or steroid (inflammation-reducing) creams, an itch that is very troublesome or that does not go away may merit a medical examination.

A symptom one should never ignore is numbness, tingling, or a pins-and-needles feeling. This can occur for a variety of reasons, including constant pressure or repetitive motion from hobbies, sports, or jobs. Tingling in the hands might come from leaning on the handlebars of a bicycle. Or it may signal nerve injury due to illness, as when the hand or foot tingles as a result of peripheral neuropathy (nerve-ending damage) caused by diabetes. Numbness and tingling can also result from such varied serious disorders as blood clots, heart attacks, tumors, or strokes (blockage of blood in the brain).

Another possible symptom of a touch disorder is pain, especially if it does not come from any detectable damage or illness. Therefore, if a person experiences a pain he or she has not experienced before that lasts a long time or keeps returning, he or she should consult a doctor to check its cause and to find ways of lessening or curing it.

•   •   •   •

CHAPTER 7

RECENT
ADVANCES

Doctors are making great progress devising techniques that repair the senses and even replace some of their parts when they become worn out, injured, or damaged by disease. A new eye surgery called radial keratotomy has been fairly successful in correcting some kinds of myopia so that the sufferer need no longer wear glasses or contact lenses. In this surgery, the doctor reshapes the cornea so that light rays entering the eye focus at the correct place on the retina.

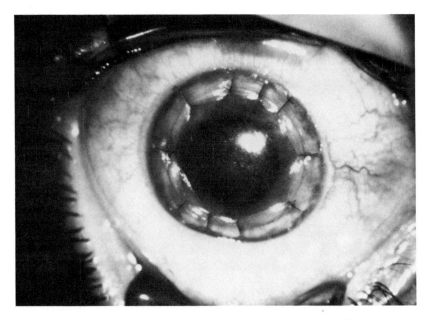

A corneal transplant. A freeze-dried cornea has been sutured onto the eye to replace a defective cornea.

Although radial keratotomy is a promising medical advance, at present it is still a controversial procedure that the American Academy of Ophthalmology has labeled experimental. More than 150,000 Americans have undergone the procedure since it was first performed in 1978; of these, according to a 1988 report from the National Eye Institute, 58% gained normal vision, whereas 26% continued to need glasses at least some of the time. In some cases, however, radial keratotomy can lead to complications, such as infection, worsened vision, and weakening of the cornea. Medical experts hope new tools will make keratotomy a much safer and more reliable procedure. For example, they have developed the laser scalpel, an instrument capable of both increasing the accuracy of surgical cuts and reducing their damage to bodily tissue.

Drs. Herbert Kaufman and Margaret McDonald have made another recent advance in the field of refractive surgery by developing a procedure called epikeratoplasty. During an epikeratoplasty a practitioner first carves and shapes a "freeze-dried" cornea, called a lenticle, to resemble a contact lens. Then a doctor stitches this cornea to the surface of the eye, as if it were a nonremovable contact lens, in an operation that has proved much simpler than the one needed for a full corneal transplant.

Although the eye's own lens is not transplantable from one person to another, this part of the eye can be replaced with a clear acrylic substitute. The recipient of an artificial lens might still require glasses to sharpen his or her near or far vision, but these implants are successful more than 95% of the time.

NEW HOPE FOR THE HEARING IMPAIRED

Procedures that replace parts of the ear with artificial implants to restore hearing are now available for those who suffer conductive deafness resulting from a ruptured eardrum, repeated infections, or damage to bones within the ear. The XOMED Audiant Bone Conductor, approved by the U.S. Food and Drug Administration in 1987, uses an implanted metal magnet to hold a sound processor tightly to the skull. This device detours sound around the damaged eardrum and bones and directs it to the inner ear, which sends it to the nerves.

An even more advanced device called the cochlear implant involves a tiny microphone-transmitter worn over the ear along with a receiver-processor implanted within the ear itself. The receiver changes sound to electrical signals and sends the signals along 22 thin implanted wires to the nerve endings in the inner ear. It is able to restore at least partial hearing to about 50% of conductive-deafness sufferers.

ADVANCES FOR THE SENSE OF TOUCH

At present, it is rarely possible to restore the sense of touch to body parts that have lost it through injury or disease because loss of touch often results from nerve damage, and nerves are extremely difficult to repair. But nerve transplants may eventually become possible if scientists can perfect the methods of reconnecting them. Doctors Louis de Medinacelli and W. J. Freed at the National Institute of Mental Health in Bethesda, Maryland, have reattached severed nerves in the legs of some animals, and Montreal researcher Dr. Albert Aguayo of McGill University has restored sight to fish whose optic nerve has been cut. Although currently in the experimental phase, such work may eventually provide not only touch sensations but also movement and possibly even sight.

Easing or eliminating the unpleasant touch sensations of pain has been a goal of doctors for all of recorded history. However, only in the past 20 years have doctors begun to have actual remedies for pain at their disposal. One method of pain control is called TENS (transcutaneous electric nerve stimulation). It uses electrodes attached to skin in painful areas to send a safe, low-level electrical current into the body. The pain is blocked because the pain nerves, preoccupied with carrying the electrical current, stop relaying pain messages to the brain.

New painkilling drugs also offer hope to pain sufferers: Studies by Dr. Jon Levine at the University of California at San Francisco show that substances called bradykinin blockers may prevent pain. Bradykinins are pain-increasing substances released when tissue is injured; when they are blocked, nerves are less sensitive to pain messages. Levine's work with bradykinin blockers has had good results in animals, and he hopes to begin testing them on human beings soon.

Nondrug methods are proving useful in combating pain as well. Three-fourths of severe-headache sufferers who have tried a method called biofeedback, in which they learn to relax, breathe deeply, and direct blood flow away from the head, have reported at least partial relief from their head pain.

SMELL AND TASTE

Because scientists still have so much to discover about the senses of smell and taste, doctors have not yet found many ways to help people who suffer from disorders of these senses. "Phantom" tastes, the mistaken sensation that there is something on the tongue tasting bitter, salty, or otherwise unpleasant, is one of the most troublesome of taste-sensation complaints. Some sufferers seem to have small seizures in the brain's taste center; others may be experiencing reactions to medicine they are taking. But so far, researchers have been unable to specify either the cause or the cure for this problem.

Similarly, people who notice strange smells that are not really there or who cannot smell anything at all remain medical mysteries. Some suffer from allergies, nerve damage, or reactions to medicine, but for others there is no identifiable cause for their difficulty. Taste researcher Dr. Linda Bartoshuk of Yale University is at present directing her research toward the study of genetic differences in the ways people taste different substances. She hopes to discover how the nervous system processes taste information, a subject about which there is currently very little known.

EXTRASENSORY PERCEPTION: THE SIXTH SENSE

Scientists have generally accepted that the five senses are the only known human means of perception. Nonetheless, many among the general population either believe in or speculate about

A cochlear implant. The disk-shaped internal receiver (left) is implanted in the skin behind the ear. One wire extends to the inner ear (represented by the model at right). An electrical current passes between the first wire and the second one, at the entrance to the inner ear, causing the hearing nerve to produce an impulse the brain perceives as sound.

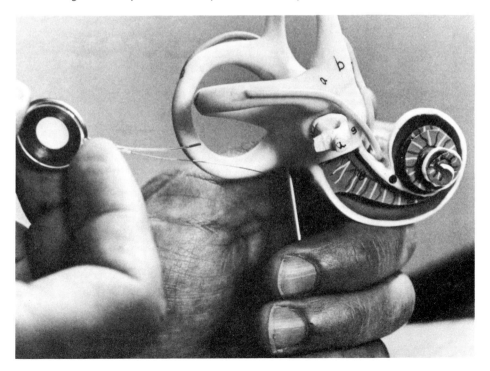

extrasensory perception (ESP), the ability to "read minds" or perceive things a person has no physical way of knowing.

People may believe in ESP for a variety of reasons: Because it is fun to imagine what it would be like for an ordinary person to have extraordinary "mental powers," some people may think they have had an ESP experience if they correctly guess who the caller will be before picking up a ringing telephone. Others claim they can predict the future, read a person's mind, or contact the dead as a dishonest way to make money.

But regardless of why people may choose to give credence to extrasensory perception, at present scientists have found no solid, verifiable proof of its existence. If ESP did exist, it would be remarkable and fascinating, but until reliable evidence for it turns up, it is possible to base actions and decisions only on information provided by those senses that are known to exist.

The sensory system has fascinated humankind since the beginning of history, but only in recent years have scientists begun to unravel some of the mysteries of how the five senses work and to explore the intricate ways in which the brain creates one's entire sensory experience from the messages the senses relay through the body to the mind. Although many aspects of this system have yet to be understood, medicine today is better able to preserve the five senses and treat them when something goes wrong than at any previous time in history.

•   •   •   •

APPENDIX:
FOR MORE INFORMATION

The following is a list of organizations that can provide further information on vision, hearing, smell, taste, and touch.

GENERAL

National Health Information Center
Office of Disease Prevention and
  Health Promotion
U.S. Department of Health and
  Human Services, Public Health
  Service
P.O. Box 1133
Washington, DC 20013-1133
(800) 336-4797
(301) 565-4167

HEARING

American Speech-Language-
  Hearing Association
10801 Rockville Pike
Rockville, MD 20852
(301) 897-5700

Canadian Association for the Deaf
271 Spadina Road, 3rd Floor
Toronto, Ontario M5R 2V3
Canada
(416) 928-1350

Canadian Hard of Hearing
  Association
2125 West 7th Avenue
Vancouver, British Columbia
V6K 1X9
Canada
(604) 731-8010

Canadian Hearing Society
271 Spadina Road
Toronto, Ontario M5R 2V3
Canada
(416) 964-9595

National Association for Hearing
  and Speech Action
10801 Rockville Pike
Rockville, MD 20852
(800) 638-8255
(301) 897-8682

The Better Hearing Institute
Box 1840
Washington, DC 20013
(703) 642-0580
Hearing Helpline:
(800) 424-8576

SMELL AND TASTE

Clinical Olfactory Research Center
Physiology Department
SUNY Health Science Center
Syracuse, NY 13210
(315) 464-5591

Connecticut Chemosensory
  Chemical Research Center
University of Connecticut Health
  Center
School of Dental Medicine
Department of BioStructure and
  Function

89

Farmington, CT 06032
(203) 679-3354
(203) 679-4082

Department of Otolaryngology and
 Maxillofacial Surgery
University of Cincinnati Medical
 Center
231 Bethesda Avenue
ML 528
Cincinnati, OH 45267-0528
(513) 558-6178
(513) 558-4048

Monell Chemical Senses Center
3500 Market Street
Philadelphia, PA 19104
(215) 898-6666

Smell and Taste Center
University of Pennsylvania
5 Ravdin Building
3400 Spruce Street
Philadelphia, PA 19104
(215) 662-6580

University of Colorado School of
 Medicine
4200 East Ninth Avenue
Denver, CO 80262
(303) 270-7988

TOUCH

American Academy of Neurology
2221 University Avenue SE
Suite 335
Minneapolis, MN 55414
(612) 623-8115

Canadian Neurological Coalition
c/o Banting Institute
100 College Street
Suite 126
Toronto, Ontario M5G 1L5
Canada
(416) 596-7043

National Chronic Pain Outreach
 Association, Inc.
8222 Wycliffe Court

Manassas, VA 22110
(703) 368-7357

VISION

American Council of the Blind
1010 Vermont Avenue NW
Suite 1100
Washington, DC 20005
(202) 393-3666
(800) 424-8666

Canadian Council of the Blind
96 Ridout Street, South
London, Ontario N6C 3X4
Canada
(519) 434-4339

Canadian National Institute for the
 Blind
1931 Bayview Avenue
Toronto, Ontario M4G 4C8
Canada
(416) 480-7580

Foundation for Glaucoma Research
490 Post Street
Suite 830
San Francisco, CA 91402
(415) 986-3162

National Society to Prevent
 Blindness
500 East Remington Road
Schaumburg, IL 60173
(312) 843-2020
(800) 331-2020

Retinitis Pigmentosa Eye Research
Suite 411
185 Spadina Avenue
Toronto, Ontario M4T 2C6
Canada
(416) 598-4951

Retinitis Pigmentosa Foundation
 Fighting Blindness
1401 Mount Royal Avenue
4th Floor
Baltimore, MD 21217
(800) 638-2300
(301) 225-9400

STATE LISTINGS

The following is a list of ophthalmology and otolaryngology departments at medical colleges in the United States.

ALABAMA

Department of Ophthalmology
University of Alabama at
  Birmingham
EFH-1
University Station
Birmingham, AL 35294
(205) 934-2014

Division of Otorhinolaryngology
University of Alabama at
  Birmingham
OHB 345
University Station
Birmingham, AL 35294
(205) 934-9765

ARIZONA

Department of Ophthalmology
University of Arizona College of
  Medicine
Arizona Health Sciences Center
1501 North Campbell Avenue
Tucson, AZ 85724

Department of Otorhinolaryngology
University of Arizona College of
  Medicine
Arizona Health Sciences Center
1501 North Campbell Avenue
Tucson, AZ 85724
(602) 626-0111

ARKANSAS

Department of Ophthalmology
University of Arkansas College of
  Medicine
4301 West Markham Street
Slot 523
Little Rock, AR 72205
(501) 661-5150

Department of Otolaryngology
University of Arkansas College of
  Medicine

4301 West Markham Street
Slot 543
Little Rock, AR 72205
(501) 661-5140

CALIFORNIA

Department of Ophthalmology
University of Southern California
  School of Medicine
2025 Zonal Avenue
Los Angeles, CA 90033
(213) 224-7167

Division of Ophthalmology
Stanford University Medical Center
Stanford, CA 94305
(415) 723-5517

Jules Stein Eye Institute
University of California
800 Westwood Plaza
Los Angeles, CA 90024
(213) 825-6089
(an RP Center that receives support
  from the RP Foundation Fighting
  Blindness)

University of California
Los Angeles School of Medicine
Department of Otolaryngology
Los Angeles, CA 90024
(213) 825-9111

COLORADO

Department of Ophthalmology
University of Colorado School of
  Medicine
4200 East Ninth Avenue
Denver, CO 80262
(303) 399-1211

Department of Otolaryngology
University of Colorado School of
  Medicine
4200 East Ninth Avenue, B-210

Denver, CO 80262
(303) 399-1211

CONNECTICUT

Department of Otolaryngology
University of Connecticut Health
  Center
Farmington, CT 06032
(203) 785-2593

Yale Eye Center
Yale University School of Medicine
333 Cedar Street
New Haven, CT 06510
(203) 785-2731

DISTRICT OF COLUMBIA

Department of Ophthalmology
Georgetown University School of
  Medicine
3900 Reservoir Road NW
Washington, DC 20007
(202) 625-7121

Department of Ophthalmology
Howard University College of
  Medicine
520 West Street NW
Washington, DC 20059
(202) 745-1257

Otolaryngology Division
George Washington University
Medical Center
2150 Pennsylvania Avenue NW
Washington, DC 20007
(202) 676-5550

FLORIDA

Bascom-Palmer Eye Institute
University of Miami School of
  Medicine
Department of Ophthalmology
900 NW 17th Street
Miami, FL 33136
(305) 326-6319
(an RP Center that receives support
  from the RP Foundation Fighting
  Blindness)

Department of Ophthalmology
University of Florida College of
  Medicine
Box J-215, J. Hillis Miller Health
  Center
Gainesville, FL 32610
(904) 392-3451

Division of Otolaryngology
University of South Florida
College of Medicine
James A. Haley Veterans Hospital
13000 North 30th Street, Room
  112-A
Tampa, FL 33612
(813) 972-7585

GEORGIA

Department of Otolaryngology
Medical College of Georgia
Augusta, GA 30912
(404) 828-2047

Emory Eye Center
Emory University School of
  Medicine
1365 Clifton Road NE
Atlanta, GA 30322
(404) 321-0111

ILLINOIS

Department of Ophthalmology
Northwestern University Medical
  School
303 East Chicago Avenue
Chicago, IL 60611
(312) 908-8649

Section of Otolaryngology
University of Chicago Medical
  Center
5841 South Maryland Avenue
Chicago, IL 60612
(312) 996-7000

University of Illinois Eye and Ear
  Infirmary
1855 West Taylor Street
Chicago, IL 60612
(312) 996-8938

(an RP Center that receives support from the RP Foundation Fighting Blindness)

INDIANA

Department of Ophthalmology
Indiana University Medical Center
702 Rotary Circle
Indianapolis, IN 46223
(317) 264-8129

Department of Otolaryngology
Indiana University Medical Center
Riley Hospital for Children, A56
702 Barnhill Drive
Indianapolis, IN 46223
(317) 630-8954

IOWA

Department of Ophthalmology
University of Iowa College of
   Medicine
100 College of Medicine
   Administration Building
Iowa City, IA 52242
(319) 353-4843

Department of Otolaryngology
University of Iowa Hospitals
Iowa City, IA 52242
(319) 356-1616

KANSAS

Department of Ophthalmology
University of Kansas Medical
   Center
School of Medicine
39th and Rainbow Blvd.
Kansas City, KS 66103
(913) 588-6600

KENTUCKY

Department of Ophthalmology
University of Kentucky College of
   Medicine
800 Rose Street
Lexington, KY 40536
(606) 233-5000

Otolaryngology Section
Department of Surgery
University of Louisville School of
   Medicine
Louisville, KY 40292
(502) 588-6994

LOUISIANA

Department of Ophthalmology
Tulane University School of
   Medicine
1430 Tulane Avenue
New Orleans, LA 70112
(504) 588-5312

Department of Otolaryngology
Louisiana State University School
   of Medicine in Shreveport
P.O. Box 33932
Shreveport, LA 71130
(318) 674-6180

MARYLAND

Department of Ophthalmology
Johns Hopkins University School of
   Medicine
720 Rutland Avenue
Baltimore, MD 21205
(301) 955-5000

Department of Otolaryngology
University of Maryland Hospital
22 Greene Street
Room 4-1181
Baltimore, MD 21201
(301) 528-2121

MASSACHUSETTS

Berman-Gund Laboratory for the
   Study of Retinal Degenerations
Massachusetts Eye and Ear
   Infirmary
Harvard Medical School
243 Charles Street
Boston, MA 02114
(617) 573-3621
(an RP Center that receives support from the RP Foundation Fighting Blindness)

Department of Ophthalmology
Tufts University School of Medicine
New England Medical Center
171 Harrison Avenue
Boston, MA 02111
(617) 956-5485

Department of Otolaryngology
Boston University Hospital
75 East Newton Street
Boston, MA 02118
(617) 247-5000

MICHIGAN

Department of Ophthalmology
University of Michigan Medical
    Center
W. K. Kellogg Eye Center
1000 Wall Street
Ann Arbor, MI 48105
(313) 763-5874

Department of Otolaryngology
Wayne State University School of
    Medicine
540 East Canfield Ave.
Detroit, MI 48201
(313) 577-0804

MINNESOTA

Department of Ophthalmology
University of Minnesota Medical
    School
Box 293 UMHC
Minneapolis, MN 55455
(612) 625-4400

Department of Otolaryngology
University of Minnesota Medical
    School
Box 396 UMHC
Minneapolis, MN 55455
(612) 625-3200

MISSISSIPPI

Department of Ophthalmology
University of Mississippi Medical
    Center
Jackson, MS 39216
(601) 984-5020

Department of Otolaryngology
University of Mississippi Medical
    Center
Jackson, MS 39216
(601) 984-5160

MISSOURI

Department of Ophthalmology
Washington University School of
    Medicine
660 South Euclid Avenue
St. Louis, MO 63110
(314) 362-7156

Department of Otolaryngology
St. Louis University School of
    Medicine
1325 South Grand Blvd.
St. Louis, MO 63101
(314) 577-8887

NEBRASKA

Department of Ophthalmology
University of Nebraska College of
    Medicine
42nd Street and Dewey Avenue
Omaha, NE 68105
(402) 559-4276

Department of Otolaryngology
Creighton University School of
    Medicine
California at 24th Street
Omaha, NE 68178
(402) 449-6501

NEW HAMPSHIRE

Department of Ophthalmology
Dartmouth Medical School
Hanover, NH 03756
(603) 646-7505

NEW JERSEY

Department of Ophthalmology
New Jersey Medical School
150 Bergen Street
Newark, NJ 07103
(201) 456-4300

Department of Otolaryngology
University of Medicine and
   Dentistry of New Jersey
Robert Wood Johnson Medical
   Center
1150 Amboy Avenue
Edison, NJ 08837
(201) 548-3200

NEW MEXICO

Department of Ophthalmology
University of New Mexico School of
   Medicine
Albuquerque, NM 87131
(505) 277-4151

NEW YORK

College of Physicians and Surgeons
Columbia University
Department of Ophthalmology
630 West 168th Street
New York, NY 10032
(212) 305-5688
(an RP Center that receives support
   from the RP Foundation Fighting
   Blindness)

Department of Ophthalmology
Cornell University Medical College
1300 York Avenue
New York, NY 10021
(212) 472-5293

Department of Ophthalmology
University of Rochester Medical
   Center
601 Elmwood Avenue
Rochester, NY 14642
(716) 275-3256

Department of Otolaryngology
Albany Medical College
47 New Scotland Avenue
Albany, NY 12208
(518) 445-3125

New York University Medical
   Center
Department of Ophthalmology
530 First Avenue

New York, NY 10016
(212) 340-6435
(an RP Center that receives support
   from the RP Foundation Fighting
   Blindness)

NORTH CAROLINA

Department of Ophthalmology
Duke University Medical Center
Box 3005
Durham, NC 27710
(919) 758-5800

Department of Ophthalmology
University of North Carolina at
   Chapel Hill
School of Medicine
Chapel Hill, NC 27514
(919) 966-5296

Department of Otolaryngology
Bowman Gray School of Medicine
Wake Forest University
300 South Hawthorne Road
Winston-Salem, NC 27103
(919) 748-4161

NORTH DAKOTA

Department of Ophthalmology
University of North Dakota School
   of Medicine
Grand Forks, ND 58202
(701) 780-6000

OHIO

Department of Ophthalmology
University of Cincinnati Medical
   Center
231 Bethesda Avenue
Cincinnati, OH 45267-0527
(513) 872-5151

Department of Otolaryngology
Case Western Reserve University
   School of Medicine
University Hospitals of Cleveland
2074 Abington Road
Cleveland, OH 44106
(216) 844-3001

OKLAHOMA

Department of Ophthalmology
University of Oklahoma Health
 Sciences Center
P.O. Box 26901
Oklahoma City, OK 73190
(405) 271-4066

Department of Otorhinolaryngology
University of Oklahoma Health
 Sciences Center
P.O. Box 26307
Oklahoma City, OK 73190
(405) 271-5504

OREGON

Department of Ophthalmology
Oregon Health Sciences University
 School of Medicine
3181 SW Sam Jackson Park Road
Portland, OR 97201
(503) 225-8311
(503) 225-8386 for RP Center that
 receives support from the RP
 Foundation Fighting Blindness

PENNSYLVANIA

Department of Ophthalmology
Hospital of the University of
 Pennsylvania
3400 Spruce Street
Philadelphia, PA 19104
(215) 662-2762

Department of Ophthalmology
Temple University
School of Medicine
3400 North Broad Street
Philadelphia, PA 19140
(215) 221-4046

Department of Otolaryngology
Pennsylvania State University
 College of Medicine
Milton S. Hershey Medical Center
Hershey, PA 17033
(717) 531-8521

SOUTH CAROLINA

Department of Ophthalmology
Medical University of South
 Carolina
171 Ashley Avenue
Charleston, SC 29425
(803) 792-2492

Department of Otolaryngology
University of South Carolina School
 of Medicine
Columbia, SC 29208
(803) 254-4158

SOUTH DAKOTA

Department of Ophthalmology
University of South Dakota School
 of Medicine
2501 West 22nd Street
Sioux Falls, SD 57105
(605) 665-9638

TENNESSEE

Department of Ophthalmology
Vanderbilt University Medical
 Center
1161 21st Avenue, South
Nashville, TN 37232
(615) 322-2031

Department of Otolaryngology
University of Tennessee, Memphis
College of Medicine
956 Court Avenue, B226
Memphis, TN 38163
(901) 528-5885

TEXAS

Cullen Eye Institute
Baylor College of Medicine
6501 Fannin, Room C109
Houston, TX 77030
(713) 799-5933
(an RP Center that receives support
 from the RP Foundation Fighting
 Blindness)

Department of Ophthalmology
University of Texas Southwestern
   Medical School at Dallas
5323 Harry Hines Boulevard
Dallas, TX 75235
(214) 688-3111

Department of Otolaryngology
University of Texas Medical Branch
John Sealy Hospital
Galveston, TX 77550
(409) 761-1011

Hermann Eye Center
University of Texas Health Science
   Center
7th Floor, Jones Pavilion
6411 Fannin
Houston, TX 77030
(713) 797-1777
(an RP Center that receives support
   from the RP Foundation Fighting
   Blindness)

UTAH

Department of Ophthalmology
University of Utah School of
   Medicine
50 North Medical Drive
Salt Lake City, UT 84132
(801) 581-6384

VERMONT

Department of Ophthalmology
University of Vermont College of
   Medicine
Burlington, VT 05405
(802) 656-4516

Department of Otolaryngology
Medical Center Hospital of
   Vermont
1 South Prospect Street
Burlington, VT 05401
(802) 656-4535

VIRGINIA

Department of Ophthalmology
University of Virginia School of
   Medicine

Box 395, Medical Center
Charlottesville, VA 22908
(804) 924-0211

Department of Otolaryngology
University of Virginia Medical
   Center
P.O. Box 430
Charlottesville, VA 22908
(804) 924-0211

WASHINGTON

Department of Ophthalmology
University of Washington School of
   Medicine, RJ-10
Seattle, WA 98195
(206) 543-3883

Department of Otolaryngology
University of Washington School of
   Medicine, RL-30
Seattle, WA 98195
(206) 543-5230

WEST VIRGINIA

Department of Ophthalmology
Marshall University School of
   Medicine
Huntington, WV 25701
(304) 526-0530

West Virginia University Medical
   Center
Department of Otolaryngology
Morgantown, WV 26506
(304) 293-0111

WISCONSIN

Department of Ophthalmology
University of Wisconsin Medical
   School
1300 University Avenue
Madison, WI 53706
(608) 263-4900

Department of Otolaryngology
Medical College of Wisconsin
Clement J. Zablocki VA Medical
   Center
5000 West National Avenue

Milwaukee, WI 53295
(414) 384-2000

CANADIAN LISTINGS

ALBERTA

Department of Ophthalmology
2-129 Clinical Sciences Building
University of Alberta
Edmonton, Alberta T6G 2G3
Canada
(403) 492-6641

MANITOBA

Department of Ophthalmology
GH-604, 820 Sherbrook Street
University of Manitoba
Winnipeg, Manitoba R3A 1R9
Canada
(204) 787-3717

ONTARIO

Department of Ophthalmology
Etherington Hall
Queen's University
Kingston, Ontario K7L 3N6

Canada
(613) 545-2559

Department of Ophthalmology
Toronto Western Hospital
399 Bathurst Street
East Wing, Room 511
Toronto, Ontario M5T 2S8
Canada
(416) 978-2634

QUEBEC

Department of Ophthalmology
Royal Victoria Hospital
McGill University
Room 8753
687 Pine Avenue, West
Montreal, Quebec H3A 1A1
Canada
(514) 842-1231

SASKATCHEWAN

Department of Ophthalmology
University of Saskatchewan
c/o University Hospital
Eye Department
Saskatoon, Saskatchewan S7N 0X0
Canada
(306) 966-8045

FURTHER READING

GENERAL

Barlow, Horace Basil. *The Senses.* New York: Cambridge University Press, 1982.

Gonzalez-Crussi, F. *The Five Senses.* San Diego: Harcourt Brace Jovanovich, 1989.

Restak, Richard. *The Brain.* New York: Bantam Books, 1984.

Rivlin, Robert. *Deciphering the Senses: The Expanding World of Human Perception.* New York: Simon & Schuster, 1984.

HEARING

Altschuler, Richard A. *Neurobiology of Hearing: The Cochlea.* New York: Raven Press, 1986.

Daniloff, Raymond. *The Physiology of Speech and Hearing: An Introduction.* Englewood Cliffs, NJ: Prentice-Hall, 1980.

Gulick, Walter Lawrence. *Hearing: Physiological Acoustics, Neural Coding, and Psychoacoustics.* New York: Oxford University Press, 1989.

Handel, Stephen. *Listening: An Introduction to the Perception of Auditory Events.* Cambridge: MIT Press, 1989.

Lutman, M. E. *Hearing Science and Hearing Disorders.* New York: Academic Press, 1983.

Miller, Aage R. *Auditory Physiology.* New York: Academic Press, 1982.

Palmer, John Milton. *Anatomy for Speech and Hearing.* 3d ed. New York: Harper & Row, 1984.

Schubert, Earl D. *Hearing: Its Function and Dysfunction.* New York: Springer-Verlag, 1980.

Skinner, Paul H. *Speech, Language, and Hearing: Normal Processes and Disorders.* 2d ed. New York: Wiley, 1985.

Yost, William A. *Fundamentals of Hearing: An Introduction.* 2d ed. New York: Holt, Rinehart & Winston, 1985.

SMELL AND TASTE

Cagan, Robert H. *Neural Mechanisms in Taste*. Boca Raton, FL: CRC Press, 1989.

Carterette, Edward C. *Tasting and Smelling*. New York: Academic Press, 1978.

Finger, Thomas E. *Neurobiology of Taste and Smell*. New York: Wiley, 1987.

Laing, David George. *Perception of Complex Smells and Tastes*. New York: Academic Press, 1989.

Wright, Robert Hamilton. *The Sense of Smell*. Boca Raton, FL: CRC Press, 1982.

TOUCH

Carterette, Edward C. *Feeling and Hurting*. New York: Academic Press, 1978.

Katz, David. *The World of Touch*. Hillsdale, NJ: Erlbaum, 1989.

Kruger, Lawrence. *Neural Mechanisms of Pain*. New York: Raven Press, 1984.

Millington, P. F. *Skin*. New York: Cambridge University Press, 1983.

Price, Donald. *Psychological and Neural Mechanisms of Pain*. New York: Raven Press, 1988.

Schiff, William. *Tactual Perception: A Sourcebook*. New York: Cambridge University Press, 1982.

Sternbach, Richard A. *Mastering Pain*. New York: Putnam, 1987.

VISION

Dobree, John H., and Eric Boulter. *Blindness and Visual Handicap: The Facts*. New York: Oxford University Press, 1982.

Glasspool, Michael. *Eyes: Their Problems and Treatments*. New York: Arco, 1987.

Heckenlively, John R., et al. *Retinitis Pigmentosa*. Philadelphia: Lippincott, 1987.

Hubel, David. *Eye, Brain, and Vision*. San Francisco: Freeman, 1988.

Marr, David. *Vision*. San Francisco: Freeman, 1983.

Simon, Hilda. *Sight and Seeing: A World of Light and Color*. New York: Putnam, 1983.

Weale, R. A. *Focus on Vision*. Cambridge: Harvard University Press, 1983.

GLOSSARY

acoustic nerve auditory nerve that connects the inner ear with the brain and carries nerve impulses to the brain

allergy a disorder in the body's immune system in which a person becomes hypersensitive to and creates antibodies against usually neutral particles (allergens) such as dust, pollen, and certain foods; these antibodies produce side effects which range in severity from sneezing to potential loss of senses

amblyopia impairment of vision causing dimness of sight in one eye without apparent change in eye structure; also known as lazy eye

amygdala one of the four basal ganglia in each cerebral hemisphere that consists of an almond-shaped mass of gray matter; this limbic system structure regulates emotions

anosmia loss or impairment of smell

biofeedback the conscious monitoring of information about usually unconscious bodily processes, such as heart rate and blood pressure; a method by which patients learn to exert some control over these internal processes; learning to relax the nervous system may relieve stress and possible pain

bradykinin a substance, composed of nine amino acids, that stimulates pain receptors; when bradykinin is blocked, nerves are less sensitive to pain messages

cerebral cortex six densely structured layers of cells that form the upper and outer portion of the brain; responsible for higher mental functions, behavioral reactions, general movement, perception, and abstract thinking

ciliary muscle an eye muscle that contracts and expands to adjust lens shape in a process known as visual accommodation

cochlea part of the ear coiled into the shape of a snail shell; forms a spiral canal with membranes, ducts, and nerves; this organ is essential to the sense of hearing

cone retinal cell that serves light and color vision; numbering between 6 million and 7 million, cones are found mainly in the macula lutea

corpuscle a small mass or body of specialized cells

depth perception the proper recognition of depth or relative distances of different objects in space

dyslexia a term used to describe a learning disorder involving written or spoken language and characterized by extreme difficulty learning and remembering letters, written or spoken words, and individual letter sounds

eustachian tube a mucous-lined auditory tube connecting the middle ear to the nose and mouth

extrasensory perception ESP; the ability to "read minds" or perceive things a person has no physical way of knowing from previous experience; commonly called the sixth sense, ESP is the object of widespread controversy and debate

glaucoma a group of eye diseases characterized by an increase in pressure inside the eye, especially on the retina and optic nerve, generally caused by a buildup of aqueous humor in the front of the eye; unless medically treated, glaucoma causes progressive sight erosion and blindness

hearing impairment damage or loss of the ability to perceive sounds; examples of such impairments are: otosclerosis (abnormal growth of tissue around the bones of the middle ear), labyrinthitis (inner ear infection), and Meniere's disease (abundance of fluid in the inner ear canals); modern surgical procedures are often able to correct hearing impairments

hippocampus a curved, elongated ridge consisting of gray matter; part of the limbic system, this area processes emotions and memories and regulates the brain's interpretation of sensory signals

human perception the understanding of how the mind turns raw electrochemical input that it receives from nerves and sense organs into a sensation that one actually experiences

hyperopia farsightedness; a condition of minimal refractive power characterized by the inability to see close objects clearly

inner ear structure fluid-filled structure that contains the cochlea and the organ of Corti (hair-cell receptors); the inner ear is responsible for balance, equilibrium, and transmission of sound waves to the brain

limbic system a group of brain structures in the parietal lobes and near the thalamus; concerned with autonomic functions and certain aspects of emotions and behavior

lobes five sensory regions within the brain that process sensory input; four lobes are contained in the cerebral hemispheres: prefrontal and frontal (movement and speech), parietal (touch), occipital (vision), and temporal (hearing); the fifth, the olfactory lobe, is located in the lower surface of the brain and processes the sense of smell

macula lutea an irregular yellowish depression on the retina's center, about three degrees wide; it is thought that its variation in size, shape, and coloring may relate to variant types of color vision

macular degeneration loss of central vision in both eyes due to retinal damage by heat from light; symptoms occur most commonly in elderly people

melanocyte an epidermal cell that produces melanin, the color-producing pigment in skin

middle ear structure contains the ear bones (hammer, anvil, and stirrup) and conducts sound waves to the inner ear; also includes muscles that protect the ear from sudden loud noises

myopia nearsightedness; the condition of unduly increased refraction by the eyes' inner structures, resulting in the inability to see distant objects clearly

nervous system the organic system that, in conjunction with the endocrine system, is responsible for the adjustments and reactions of an organism to internal and environmental conditions; the central nervous system consists of the brain and the spinal cord; the peripheral nervous system registers physical sensations, such as temperature and pain; the autonomic nervous system is divided into two parts: the sympathetic nervous system, which mobilizes outgoing energy and governs the body's reactions to arousal and external stimuli, and the parasympathetic nervous system, which maintains such internal bodily processes as energy storage, relaxation, and nourishment

neurotransmitter a chemical that transmits nerve impulses across a synapse

nociception the reaction of nerve endings due to injury; nerves in the damaged area signal distress to the brain

olfaction/olfactory having to do with the processes of smelling

outer ear structure containing the eardrum, or tympanic membrane, this structure is responsible for the reception of external sound waves

peripheral neuropathy nerve-ending damage

peripheral vision what the eye sees at the far right, left, top, or bottom edges of its scope of vision

pheromones chemicals perceived through the olfactory system and thought to have an effect on the reproductive behavior of animals and humans

radial keratotomy corrective surgery used for myopia, in which the cornea is reshaped so that light rays focus on the correct place on the retina

rod retinal cell that serves night vision and motion detection; numbering approximately 12 million, most rods are located on the periphery of the retina

sensory illusions an alteration of the original sensory information caused by a conflict in the processing of that information in the brain

strabismus heterotropia; squint; a condition in which one eyeball, and accordingly its field of vision, deviates from the other eye and its focus; usually caused by an imbalance of eyeball muscles

synapse the point of contact where nerve impulses are transmitted from one neuron to another

taste buds any of the cells in the tongue that are sense organs of taste

touch-sensory pathways the route along which nerve messages travel; for example, the spinothalamic route is the pair of main nerve tracts along the spinal cord responsible for pain and temperature sensations

transcutaneous electric nerve stimulation TENS; a method of pain control using electrodes attached to painful areas of the skin and through which a safe low-level electrical current is sent into the body; the pain is blocked because the pain nerves, involved with the transport of the current into the body, stop sending pain messages to the brain

INDEX

PICTURE CREDITS

Mary Kittredge, a former associate editor of the medical journal *Respiratory Care*, is now a free-lance writer of nonfiction and fiction. Her writing awards include the Ruell Crompton Tuttle Essay Prize and the Mystery Writers of America Robert L. Fish Award for best first short-mystery fiction of 1986. She received a B.A. from Trinity College in Hartford, Connecticut, and studied at the University of California Medical Center, San Francisco. She is certified as a respiratory-care technician by the American Association for Respiratory Therapy and has been a member of the respiratory-care staff at Yale–New Haven Hospital and Medical Center since 1972.

Dale C. Garell, M.D., is medical director of California Children Services, Department of Health Services, County of Los Angeles. He is also associate dean for curriculum at the University of Southern California School of Medicine and clinical professor in the Department of Pediatrics & Family Medicine at the University of Southern California School of Medicine. From 1963 to 1974, he was medical director of the Division of Adolescent Medicine at Children's Hospital in Los Angeles. Dr. Garell has served as president of the Society for Adolescent Medicine, chairman of the youth committee of the American Academy of Pediatrics, and as a forum member of the White House Conference on Children (1970) and White House Conference on Youth (1971). He has also been a member of the editorial board of the *American Journal of Diseases of Children*.

C. Everett Koop, M.D., Sc.D., is former Surgeon General, Deputy Assistant Secretary for Health, and Director of the Office of International Health of the U.S. Public Health Service. A pediatric surgeon with an international reputation, he was previously surgeon-in-chief of Children's Hospital of Philadelphia and professor of pediatric surgery and pediatrics at the University of Pennsylvania. Dr. Koop is the author of more than 175 articles and books on the practice of medicine. He has served as surgery editor of the *Journal of Clinical Pediatrics* and editor-in-chief of the *Journal of Pediatric Surgery*, Dr. Koop has received nine honorary degrees and numerous other awards, including the Denis Brown Gold Medal of the British Association of Paediatric Surgeons, the William E. Ladd Gold Medal of the American Academy of Pediatrics, and the Copernicus Medal of the Surgical Society of Poland. He is a Chevalier of the French Legion of Honor and a member of the Royal College of Surgeons, London.